CHILDREN OF THE PRISON BOOM

Recent Titles in

STUDIES IN CRIME AND PUBLIC POLICY

Michael Tonry and Norval Morris, General Editors

CHILDREN OF THE PRISON BOOM

Mass Incarceration and the Future of American Inequality

SARA WAKEFIELD

CHRISTOPHER WILDEMAN

OXFORD
UNIVERSITY PRESS

OXFORD
UNIVERSITY PRESS

Oxford University Press is a department of the University of Oxford.
It furthers the University's objective of excellence in research, scholarship,
and education by publishing worldwide. .

Oxford   New York
Auckland   Cape Town   Dar es Salaam   Hong Kong   Karachi
Kuala Lumpur   Madrid   Melbourne   Mexico City   Nairobi
New Delhi   Shanghai   Taipei   Toronto

With offices in
Argentina   Austria   Brazil   Chile   Czech Republic   France   Greece
Guatemala   Hungary   Italy   Japan   Poland   Portugal   Singapore
South Korea   Switzerland   Thailand   Turkey   Ukraine   Vietnam

Oxford is a registered trademark of Oxford University Press
in the UK and certain other countries.

Published in the United States of America by
Oxford University Press
198 Madison Avenue, New York, NY 10016

© Oxford University Press 2014

First issued as an Oxford University Press paperback, 2016

Library of Congress Cataloging-in-Publication Data
Wakefield, Sara.
Children of the prison boom : mass incarceration and the future of American
inequality / Sara Wakefield, Christopher Wildeman.
    pages cm. —(Studies in crime and public policy)
ISBN 978-0-19-998922-5 (hardback); 978-0-19-062459-0 (paperback)
1. Children of prisoners–United States–Social conditions.   2. Corrections–Social
aspects–United States. 3. Imprisonment–United States.   4. Equality–United States.
I. Wildeman, Christopher James, 1979-II. Title.
HV8886.U5W35 2013
362.82'950973–dc23

For Riley

*For Carol, Cilla,
Greta, Jim and Silas*

CONTENTS

ACKNOWLEDGMENTS

This book could not have been accomplished without the generous support of many, many people. We would like to acknowledge some of them here—though our gratitude extends further—and hope that the reader holds us (rather than those who us gave financial, intellectual, or emotional support) responsible for shortcomings in our work. This is our first book so we reserve the right to gush and have made no attempt to be succinct—but we promise to return to the expected pithy academic prose in the pages to follow these acknowledgments. We also hope that we can make it up to anyone we foolishly omitted. As we write, our editor likely grows impatient, so we surely will forget some people who are incredibly important to us intellectually, personally, or both. We will buy you a beer the next time we see you to make it up to you.

We first would like to direct the reader to several related publications that are foundational to the book. Although much of the analysis in this book is new, many of the earlier analyses on which it is based have appeared in other outlets (Wakefield 2007; Wakefield and Uggen 2010; Wakefield and Wildeman 2011; Wildeman 2009, 2010, 2012, Forthcoming, and Wildeman and

Muller 2012). Interested readers may want to consult these earlier works for more depth on each substantive topic as well as for additional statistical analyses. We are especially grateful to the reviewers, editors, and coauthors of those earlier works, as well as to the Oxford reviewers of the book, all of whom helped make the project what it is today.

In thanking the folks who helped this book come to fruition, we start with our dissertation committees, funders, and publisher, all of whom made this project what it is.

Our work on parental incarceration began in graduate school, where our PhD-granting departments generously supported us. Parts of the work presented here were supported by a University of Minnesota Doctoral Dissertation Fellowship, an Anna Welsch Bright Fellowship from the Department of Sociology at the University of Minnesota, and the Harry Frank Guggenheim Foundation. We are greatly indebted to our exceptional dissertation committees and mentors. Chris Uggen, Candace Kruttschnitt, Scott Eliason, and Jeylan Mortimer guided Sara's dissertation in the right direction. Bruce Western, Sara McLanahan, and Devah Pager did the same for Chris. We are especially grateful to these seven people since without our dissertations, this book likely would not exist.

Our joint work was supported by a Presidential Authority Award from the Russell Sage Foundation. We would especially like to thank Jim Wilson and Suzanne Nichols at Russell Sage for their early guidance and support. Jacob Hacker at the Institution for Social and Policy Studies at Yale University also provided some late but generous (and desperately needed) support. Guidance during the later stages of the work was provided consistently and astutely by James Cook at Oxford University Press, and for this we will forever be grateful. Because of his excellent help in broadening the scope of the original manuscript, enduring friendship, and willingness to discuss the latest Barclay's Premier League match, we cannot imagine a better editor to guide this book through the process. We hope to work with you again, James. (We also appreciate the late but strong support and encouragement of Maura Roessner at the University of California Press.)

Yet, two good dissertation committees, a handful of generous funders, some related works, and one great editor do not a book make (unless they are all willing to chip in with the writing), and we are also indebted to a number of colleagues who provided the critical feedback and emotional support necessary to get this book out. Maybe most importantly, we both received incredible support from our home departments—and universities more broadly.

In the Department of Criminology, Law and Society (CLS) at the University of California, Irvine, Sara would like to acknowledge the support and mentoring of Carroll Seron, Val Jenness, Joan Petersilia, and Jenn Earl (at Arizona) with this work (and everything else). Simon Cole and Justin Richland were also incredibly supportive, and I thank them for their friendship. I worked in a collegial and energetic environment while writing this book—the line between colleagues and friends blurred long ago. While I cannot name them all here, the faculty and graduate students of CLS all played a role in the completion of this work—whether by offering me time off to write or by challenging me with the creativity and care evident in their own research. Beyond UCI, Chris Uggen deserves special acknowledgement. Chris taught me all the important stuff, and he remains the voice in my head, cautioning me to be clear, careful, and always sure about what I "know" before I speak to my students, my colleagues, or the public at large (thankfully for the public, I do this much less frequently than Chris). Thank you to all.

In the Department of Sociology at Yale University, Chris is especially indebted to Marcus Hunter, who throughout this process has been undoubtedly his most important support of the people not tied to him by blood or marriage—or unfortunate enough to have known him before he came to Yale. Thank you, Marcus. Andy Papachristos also always had a kind word to offer, even if our conversations about this book tended to veer in the direction of the six bestsellers he was currently crafting. (Just kidding, Andy.)

Beyond these two, I am also incredibly grateful to the wildly supportive folks at the Center for Research on Inequalities and the Life Course (especially Richard Breen, Vida Maralani, Lloyd Grieger, Jennifer Flashman, and Anette Fasang) and the two political scientists who made me think big over at the Institution for Social and Policy Studies, Jacob Hacker and Vesla Weaver, as well as to Tracey Meares from the law school and Emily Wang from the medical school, both of whom mostly kept me in line. Finally, I can't say enough about the incredible support I have received from my colleagues in the Department of Sociology. So thanks to those of you I haven't mentioned yet (in alphabetical order by last name: Julia Adams, Jeff Alexander, Rene Almeling, Eli Anderson, Scott Boorman, Debbie Davis, Emily Erikson, Ron Eyerman, Phil Gorski, Phil Smith, Olav Sorenson, Peter Stamatov, and Jonathan Wyrtzen).

Beyond our home departments and institutions, we are also indebted to Chris Muller for his insightful read of an earlier version of this manuscript. He is a gifted scholar and editor and the book is much better for his comments. (Chris would also especially like to thank him for being an incredible friend throughout this whole process.) We also thank Natalia Emanuel, who gave generously of her time and creativity to produce the figures, even in the midst of her senior thesis. (Chris would also like to thank her for becoming such a great friend and collaborator over the last year.) At UCI, Charlotte Bradstreet and Alyssa Whitby-Chamberlain provided excellent research assistance for this project. (Sara would also like to thank Julie Gerlinger for skillfully taking care of all the rest of my research responsbilities when I was off writing.)

We thank the Council on Crime and Justice, Ebony Ruhland, and Ryan Dailey for their assistance to Sara in completing the qualitative interviews we used and for their work on behalf of the incarcerated and their families. We are most appreciative of all the families who allowed Sara into their homes to discuss the difficult experience of having a parent incarcerated. We are humbled by their strength, their humor, and their resilience. We hope that the pages that follow do justice to their experiences.

It became abundantly clear to us while writing this book just how lucky and privileged we are to have such a supportive network of partners (one, not multiple, each!), friends, and family. We could not have completed this work without them, and we now turn to thanking them.

Sara would like to thank Bobby Apel for keeping me out of oncoming traffic against long odds, (too) well fed, and always happy as I finished this book. I would also like to acknowlege the support of Beth and Steve Cauffman. They are treasured friends—if it takes a village to raise a child (and a dog) and if you choose your family in adulthood, they are mine, and I am quite concerned about the prospect of going it alone soon (rather, Riley should be quite concerned). Charis Kubrin, much like Beth, somehow manages to be one of my closest friends while also providing mentoring when needed. She's a hoot—and wicked smart, strategic, honorable, and generous. Thanks to the rest of the girls (Jen Lee, Francesca Polletta, Kim Putnam, Juliet Coscia, and Kristin Turney) and the boys (Ryan King, Mike Massoglia, Ed Amenta, and Thad Domina) for the advice, support, and dinners. Most importantly, I'd like to thank Chris Wildeman—a wonderful collaborator but a better friend. Can we still talk twice a day after this comes out?

Writing this book brought home just how lucky I was growing up. My parents, Patricia Ehresman and Jerry Bartlett, did all of the things that we say in the book are important for child well-being—they gave me an education, financial support, a moral center, a safety net, and stability. My stepfather, David Ehresman, and grandparents, Lorne and Ruberta Quarn, were no less important and did the same throughout my childhood and beyond. Thank you also to my brother and sister-in-law, Chris and Julia Bartlett, for all their support (not least allowing me to squat at their apartment in New York City during the initial writing of the manuscript). To my delightfully feisty, smart, beautiful, and funny daughter, Riley, it is a pleasure watching you grow up (and forgive me the many mistakes I make along the way).

Chris would like to first thank his friends who also had the misfortune of being his coauthors throughout this process (or vice versa). Kristin Turney, Jason Schnittker, and Hedy Lee were especially kind to continue working with me even when I basically stopped using any words except "ugh," "book," and "due" when they asked me about the progress of our papers. Sarah Burgard and Jeff Morenoff also deserve special mention for being such incredible mentors when I was at Michigan, although I think of them as friends as much as mentors. The usual cast of characters I don't write with but still talk to all the time (or at least as much as I can) also deserve my thanks. So big thanks to you, Ben, Buwalda, CAM, Edenbo, and Hesselink. Of course, the person who suffered through this with me most was Sara Wakefield, and for her kindness as a coauthor and friend I could not be more grateful. Thanks for making me see that writing a book was a good idea, Sara. It seems so much less horrible on this end.

Finally, I owe three generations of Wildemans more than I can ever say or repay. To start with the generation that helped least (except for keeping me sane enough or so sleep-deprived enough that I stopped caring about deadlines for an instant), I thank Greta and Silas. For putting up with all of the things that make me annoying (both book-related and not book-related) and loving me enough to not always tell me how difficult I am, I thank Cilla. I love you, honey. Finally, my parents, Jim and Carol, have supported my intellectual and personal endeavors so well over the years that it's hard to know what to fixate on most. So I will instead apologize for becoming a quantitative social scientist instead of something more interesting like a cultural anthropologist or a paleontologist. Sorry! A truly huge thanks to the five of you!

CHILDREN OF THE PRISON BOOM

INTRODUCTION

MICHAEL AND NATHANIEL were born in the early 1990s to African American single mothers. At the time of their birth, each of their fathers was in prison. Their childhoods shared many other features. Both grew up in neighborhoods decimated by the crack epidemic and, as a result, witnessed violence and drug abuse in their youth. Both attended failing public schools with inadequate resources and high dropout rates. And for both, the majority of the children in their neighborhood went on to lead lives similar to those of their parents, in which addiction, single parenthood, and incarceration were all commonplace.

If their childhood circumstances look quite similar, their later outcomes could hardly differ more. Chaos has characterized Nathaniel's life. He was expelled from school, amassed a lengthy criminal record, and, at the age of fourteen, served time in a secure juvenile detention facility. Michael's life unfolded very differently. He graduated from high school and went on to receive a bachelor's degree and a master's degree from Stanford University. As an undergraduate, he also interned at the White House. And shortly after graduating, in 2012, at the age of twenty-two, Michael became the youngest elected council member in the city of Stockton, California. Nathaniel's aunt describes his life today as "over before it's begun."[1] Michael Tubbs's story received as much attention for his accomplishments at such a young age as for the disadvantages he overcame in order to achieve them.[2]

Both of these stories resonate with us, yet for different reasons. Nathaniel's story rings true because it is what we fear but can't help expecting: he has followed in his father's footsteps. Michael's story resonates with us for a different reason. We are drawn to Michael's

2 | CHILDREN OF THE PRISON BOOM

story because moving from one end of the socioeconomic ladder to the other is so difficult, even for those who possess abundant natural skills, talents, and luck. Indeed, his story represents not what we expect but what we hope for. We all grow up being told that if we set our mind to something, we can accomplish anything. Michael is the exception that proves the rule—the model of resilience and self-belief we are told to strive for.[3]

This book is about Nathaniel, Michael, and the millions of other children of the prison boom—children who at some point experienced the imprisonment of a parent, often a father, during the period since the 1970s when the incarceration rate grew sixfold. For a few children, the experience motivates them to do better in their own lives. For most, it leads to adverse consequences that ripple from infancy throughout childhood and even adulthood. Together, Michael and Nathaniel represent both the potential for resilience and the worst-case scenario for those millions of children. In this book, we consider the lives of these children to show that an outcome like Michael's is possible but that the outcomes for typical children of the prison boom look more like Nathaniel's.

This book is also about how mass imprisonment has transformed racial inequality among children, with implications for the future of inequality in America. We find that children like Nathaniel and Michael—African Americans born around 1990 whose fathers dropped out of high school—had a better than even chance of having a father imprisoned, at 50.5 percent. We also find very high cumulative risks of paternal imprisonment for all black children born in 1990. The risk of paternal imprisonment for all African American children is about 25 percent. These risks dwarf the risks for comparable white children, suggesting that mass parental imprisonment might have increased racial inequalities among children. In the following pages, we simultaneously tell a story about individual children who suffer as a result of the incarceration of a father, as well as one about how paternal incarceration affects the American inequality we all experience.

MACRO-LEVEL CHANGE AND CHILDHOOD INEQUALITY

Economic Shifts

Children experience all sorts of things as they grow up that influence their well-being, many of which have little to do with them and everything to do with their parents. Indeed, a central question for social scientists revolves around the influence of the shifting fortunes of parents on their children (Duncan, Featherman, and Duncan 1972). To take but one example that speaks to contemporary economic conditions, research suggests problematic, long-term consequences for the children of those laid off during the recent Great Recession. Spells of parental unemployment, especially those that last a long time, have consequences for children, including increased financial instability (Holzer 2010), parental stress (Jones 1988), and even an increased risk of homelessness (Lovell and Isaacs 2010).

Economic instability also can have effects at the aggregate level, meaning that they matter not just for children who personally experience the unemployment of a parent but also for other children growing up during the same uncertain times. A now classic study by sociologist Glen Elder describes the long-term consequences of the Great Depression for entire cohorts of American children (Elder 1974, 1999), demonstrating that shifts in the social circumstances of children—events like the Great Depression or the recent "Great Recession" that began in December 2007—may profoundly affect entire cohorts of children as they grow up.

The influence of parental circumstances on the lives of children is apparent not only in differences between birth cohorts but also in long-standing racial disparities in health, educational and occupational attainment, and well-being. For example, black and white children differ on a variety of measures of social adjustment, including school readiness and high school completion (McLeod and Kaiser 2004), infant mortality (Wise 2003; Frisbie et al. 2004; Schempf et al. 2007), child homelessness (Staveteig and Wigton 2000), and teen pregnancy (Trent and Crowder 1997), all of which affect how they fare in adulthood. Social scientists have proposed a variety of explanations for these racial gaps, including differences in the risks of growing up poor, living in a poor neighborhood, and being raised by a single mom (Gortmaker and Wise 1997; McLeod and Nonnemaker 2000). None of these explanations fully explain racial disparity in these outcomes, however. We demonstrate that accounting for paternal imprisonment represents a significant advance in explaining the racial gaps in childhood well-being, and has implications not only for individual children, but also for inequality among them.

Paternal incarceration is particularly important today because, contrary to earlier periods in American history, millions of children now experience it. The influence of the prison in American life has grown greatly in the last four decades. Perhaps the best evidence of how widespread the experience of incarceration has become is found in the creation of a new Muppet in 2013 by the iconic children's show, Sesame Street. An online tool kit of resources for children of incarcerated parents accompanied the introduction of Alex, a Muppet with an incarcerated father.[4] The United States today incarcerates a larger share of its population than at any point in its history, and more than any other country. This shift has had a vast impact on American children because prison and jail inmates are parents to an estimated 2.5 million minor children, a huge increase from the 500,000 children with incarcerated parents in 1980 (Pettit 2012: 84).

Parental Imprisonment

Our decision to focus on how mass imprisonment might explain the persistent racial gaps in child well-being is motivated by three observations. First, the increase in both the number of incarcerated adults and racial disparities in the risk of imprisonment mean that many more children—especially African American children like Nathaniel and Michael—experience parental imprisonment now than would have in the not-too-distant past. Second, there are good empirical and theoretical reasons to expect that the incarceration of a parent causes problems for the average child, even if it does help a few children. Third, the harm caused by the combination of parental incarceration and the vast racial disparities in the risk of experiencing it suggests that mass imprisonment may perpetuate social inequality.

Although these three ideas are straightforward, combining and testing them is new. Scholars of disparities in child well-being have done little (if anything) to incorporate high levels of parental imprisonment into their analyses. And scholars of the prison boom have tended to focus on how imprisonment drives disparities among adult men or their romantic partners. As we show in the chapters that follow, this oversight may obscure the most powerful effects of high incarceration rates on inequality today and in the future.

At first glance, it seems reasonable to assume that the children of the prison boom would do poorly relative to other children (in a host of domains). Foundational work in criminology points toward children with criminally involved parents struggling for a number of reasons, whether their parents experienced incarceration or not (Glueck and Glueck 1950; Gottfredson and Hirschi 1990; Hirschi 1969; Nye 1958; Reckless 1961; Sampson and Laub 1993; Sutherland and Cressey 1978). What remains unclear is whether having an imprisoned parent is an independent cause of these poor outcomes. For that to be the case, the parents who experience incarceration must be connected to family life in some ways, and their incarceration must, on average, do more harm than good to their families. On the first condition, research on current and former inmates shows strong evidence of robust family ties for most, although certainly not all, of these men and women (e.g., Braman 2004; Comfort 2008; Nurse 2002). Decades of research, in part motivated by the prison boom in the United States, tells us that the image of the inmate as an isolated loner is simply false. On the second condition, there is also evidence that incarceration might do damage to family life. Inmates today are not only more often than not parents but are also less likely to be incarcerated for violent offenses and to have been unemployed prior to imprisonment than in the past. These descriptive facts underscore a research literature showing that mass imprisonment affects the labor market (Pager 2003; Western 2002), romantic partners (Comfort 2008), neighborhoods (Clear 2007), and the electoral system (Manza and Uggen 2006). Unless one is willing to argue that incarceration influences labor markets and partners but not children, there are good reasons to focus on the consequences of parental incarceration for these children.

A large, rapidly growing research literature now shows just how consequential the prison boom might be for American children, as much of it shows that the ties between parental incarceration and child well-being are global and negative, especially for paternal incarceration (see the review of Murray, Farrington, and Sekol 2012).[5] As we show in chapter 4, the evidence is particularly strong with respect to children's mental health and behavioral problems, and several studies using data sources across a variety of contexts and time periods have linked parental incarceration to negative outcomes for children (e.g., Craigie 2011; Geller et al., 2009, 2012; Johnston 1995; Kinner et al. 2007; Murray and Farrington 2005; Poehlman 2005; Stanton 1980; Wakefield and Wildeman 2011; Wilbur et al. 2007; Wildeman 2010).

Parental imprisonment is also linked with outcomes into adolescence and adulthood, further suggesting that mass imprisonment might be important for the future of American inequality. For example, research has considered the intergenerational transmission of crime and punishment, finding that parental incarceration is a significant predictor of criminal involvement, conviction, and imprisonment among adolescents and adults (Huebner and Gustafson 2007; Murray, Loeber, and Pardini 2012; Murray and Farrington 2005; Roettger and Swisher 2011; van de Rakt et al.

2012). Others studies link paternal imprisonment to substance use and abuse (Roettger et al. 2011), poor educational outcomes (Hagan and Foster 2012), and social exclusion more broadly (Foster and Hagan 2007), suggesting broad associations between paternal incarceration and adult outcomes. Taken together, the results from these studies link parental incarceration with a cascade of negative outcomes, moving from behavioral and mental health problems in childhood to early drug and alcohol use and delinquency in adolescence, and culminating in poor educational outcomes and weak attachment to prosocial institutions in early adulthood.

Though this evidence is substantial with respect to the range of outcomes and stages in the life course considered, obstacles to causal inference remain substantial, and without showing *effects* of parental imprisonment on children, we cannot make any arguments about how mass imprisonment shapes inequality (Giordano 2010; Johnson and Easterling 2012; Johnston 2006; Sampson 2011; Wildeman, Wakefield, and Turney 2013). Although there may be good reasons to think paternal incarceration influences child (and adult) outcomes and evidence suggesting such a link, the disadvantages typical of the population and the potential countervailing effects of paternal incarceration present significant challenges for the analyses in this book. We delve into these issues in greater detail in chapters 3 and 4, but note here that our choice of parents (fathers) and outcomes (children's behavioral and mental health problems, infant mortality, and child homelessness) is driven by an interest in (1) the contexts in which parental imprisonment is sufficiently common to broadly affect macro-level inequality, (2) the most proximate causes of problems during childhood, adolescence, and adulthood, and (3) the availability of data capable of isolating the effects of parental imprisonment on these outcomes. As we show later, limiting our analysis in these ways causes us to focus only on the effects of paternal incarceration on children's outcomes in the contemporary United States because it is for this narrow swath of children that the data allow us to make strong claims about effects on inequality.

To briefly outline our decision-making process in each step, we first explain our emphasis on paternal incarceration. Our focus is on the role mass incarceration plays in shaping social inequality, and the imprisonment of a father is much more common than the imprisonment of a mother. The rate of women's imprisonment has increased substantially in recent decades, but the experience remains rare, even among the most disadvantaged families; and it simply does not occur at levels high enough to drive social inequality in a meaningful way (as we demonstrate in chapter 2), though there has been much high-quality work on the consequences of maternal incarceration for child well-being (e.g., Arditti 2012; Cho 2009a, 2009b; Daillaire et al. 2010; Hagan and Foster 2012; Huebner and Gustafson 2007; Giordano 2010; Siegel 2011). That said, we suspect that the effects of maternal incarceration on children are largely dwarfed by disadvantages present prior to imprisonment (Giordano 2010; Siegel 2011), and some, though not all, rigorous work on the topic suggests null effects (Cho 2009a, 2009b; Wildeman and Turney Forthcoming). For these reasons, we focus most of our attention on father incarceration rather than mother incarceration (though chapter 2 provides estimates of the cumulative risk of maternal imprisonment and chapter 6 incorporates maternal incarceration into our analysis of the risk of child homelessness).

We also focus our attention on the contemporary United States. Excellent work links parental incarceration to negative outcomes for children in other contexts, including but not limited to the United Kingdom (e.g., Murray and Farrington 2005), the Netherlands (van de Rakt et al. 2012), and Denmark (Wildeman et al., forthcoming). But none of these works can speak to the unique effects of mass incarceration on social inequality. A number of countries have experienced large increases in their prison populations in recent years (for example, the UK and the Netherlands), but the American context is truly unique both in the sheer volume of inmates and in sustaining such large increases in imprisonment over a long period of time. Relying on studies with samples not from the United States, for instance, makes it hard to know how effects from another context translate back to the American context.[6] Of the countries with a substantial prison population and racial inequality in imprisonment, furthermore, the United States is the only one in which data make it possible to estimate the cumulative risk of paternal imprisonment, rendering it impossible to estimate the effects of incarceration on childhood inequality elsewhere.[7]

Finally, in a similar vein, we opted whenever possible to use data sets that allowed us to tie new episodes of paternal incarceration to changes in children's outcomes because this enabled us to control for stable characteristics of children and families—neighborhood context, parental self-control, and childhood temperament, for instance—which makes our estimates more credible. It is for this reason that we opted not to include the National Longitudinal Study of Adolescent Health (Add Health), which has been widely used to consider the relationship between paternal incarceration and adolescent and young adult outcomes (e.g., Foster and Hagan 2007, 2009; Roettger and Boardman 2012; Roettger and Swisher 2011; Roettger et al. 2011). These data can only tie paternal incarceration to a change in child outcomes if the father experienced a new incarceration when the child was an adolescent or young adult, a relatively rare event among Add Health participants.

We therefore focus here on two sets of consequential experiences in childhood, each of which we can analyze using broadly representative data that tell us about the contemporary American children most affected by mass imprisonment and allow us to tie changes in paternal incarceration to changes in child well-being. The first set of outcomes we consider, mental health and behavioral problems, is related to a host of key outcomes in adolescence and adulthood that we cannot study because of data limitations, including both educational (McLeod and Kaiser 2004) and occupational attainment (Mannuzza et al. 1997). Beyond effects on key points of stratification, such as educational attainment and labor market outcomes, our results for mental health and behavioral problems also speak to later criminal justice outcomes. Physical aggression in childhood, for example, one of the behavioral problems we consider, is one of the best predictors of crime and criminal justice involvement in adolescence and adulthood, if not the best (Loeber and Hay 1997; Moffitt 1993). We focus on mental health and behavioral problems because they tell us how these children will likely be doing in a range of important domains five, ten, and maybe even twenty years down the road.

We then turn our attention to outcomes that touch the lives of fewer children but in a more dramatic fashion: infant mortality and homelessness. Infant mortality represents the most tragic of incarceration effects. Yet infant mortality is important not only because it is tragic but also because the infant mortality rate is generally considered the best gauge of how healthy the average child in any society is (Wise 2003). Put simply, if you know a society's infant mortality rate, you know how healthy the children who do not pass away prematurely are as well. We focus on infant mortality not only as a representation of the fact that sometimes childhood disadvantages are so extreme that there are no adult outcomes, but also because doing so gives us insight into how the prison boom may shape inequalities in child health.

We focus on homelessness, another event we would all hope to have our children avoid, for two reasons. For one, child homelessness has durable negative consequences, meaning that its effects spill over into adulthood. Because homeless children experience high rates of victimization (Hagan and McCarthy 1997) and exposure to infectious disease (Haddad et al. 2005) and have limited access to health care (Kushel, Vittinghoff, and Haas 2001), childhood homelessness compromises later health. Homeless children struggle to keep up with their schoolwork and suffer more mental health problems (Buckner 2008; Rafferty, Shinn, and Weitzman 2004; Vostanis, Grattan, and Cumella 1997). In addition to these long-term, negative consequences, child homelessness has contributed to massive shifts in the composition of the homeless population since the mid-1980s. Classic accounts of the homeless focused on the single white men who made up the majority of this population (Bahr and Caplow 1974). Yet, starting in the early 1980s, the share of the homeless composed of African Americans and children began to grow (Hopper 2003; Lee, Tyler, and Wright 2010: 505). These shifts have led to risks of child homelessness at levels unthinkable even in the 1980s: Today, 2 percent of American children are homeless annually (National Center on Family Homelessness 2009). Racial disparities in this risk are pronounced. Black children ages 0–4 in New York City were twenty-nine to thirty-five times more likely to have stayed in a shelter in the last year than were whites, for instance (Culhane and Metraux 1999: 227–228).

Our focus on mental health and behavioral problems, infant mortality, and child homelessness is well motivated, but importantly, we exclude from our analysis the effects of parental imprisonment for outcomes in adulthood. Although our ideal analysis would consider the consequences of mass imprisonment for inequality in the educational, labor market, and criminal justice outcomes of adult children, we are forced to confine our gaze somewhat more narrowly in the interest of providing the most credible causal estimates possible in our empirical work. This means, critically, that if the effects of paternal incarceration for adult children shown in other research are causal (as we suspect many are), then we will almost certainly underestimate the influence of mass imprisonment on social inequality by omitting these effects from consideration.

Taken together, our analyses represent the first systematic analyses of the relationship between parental incarceration and social inequality, now and in the future. Students of mass incarceration have long recognized the implications of their work for inequality (Western 2006; Wakefield and Uggen 2010), but few studies have quantified the potential impact (Wildeman and Muller 2012; Western and Muller 2013). Moreover, our focus on black-white disparities across the range of outcomes we have chosen offers a glimpse into population health more generally.

The results of our analysis are not encouraging. We show that the prison has become an institution that structures inequality in much the same way that tracking does in the educational system or segmentation does in the labor market. More troubling, even if incarceration rates were reduced dramatically in the near future, the long-term harms of our national experiment in the mass incarceration of marginalized men have yet to be fully revealed, since many children of the prison boom have yet to come of age.

Yet to tell this story, we need to first explain what the prison boom is, as well as how previous research suggests it has shaped public safety and social stratification.

MASS IMPRISONMENT AND AMERICAN INEQUALITY

The extent of the relationship between imprisonment and inequality is unprecedented and largely confined to the contemporary United States. The onset of the prison boom was also accompanied by an unprecedented decline in crime in the United States. In light of this, discussions of the mass imprisonment's consequences for social inequality must be weighed against its consequences for public safety (e.g., Sampson 2011). In the next two sections, we define mass imprisonment and consider its effects on crime, before turning to its broader social consequences. The most rigorous econometric research finds that the public safety returns from imprisonment are much smaller than is widely believed and have declined over time.

Defining Mass Imprisonment

Had incarceration rates remained stable over the last few decades, parental incarceration would have remained troubling but rare. In the early 1970s, the American imprisonment rate was comparable to other developed democracies and relative to earlier periods in

American history (Blumstein and Cohen 1973). In fact, the incarceration rate had deviated so little over the previous fifty years that in 1973 eminent criminologists Alfred Blumstein and Jacqueline Cohen argued that the American incarceration rate tended to reach stability at about 100 inmates per 100,000 in the population, deviating only slightly even in the face of dramatic upheavals, such as two world wars and the Great Depression (Blumstein and Cohen 1973). Despite long-standing racial disparities in imprisonment (Muller 2012), imprisonment was still far from common, even for marginal men. Indeed, imprisonment was so rare for black men residing in poor neighborhoods that ethnographic accounts of these neighborhoods from this period mentioned it only in passing (Liebow [1967] 2003); Stack 1974).

By 2010, so much had changed. After forty years of nearly unabated growth, the American imprisonment rate is five times what it was in the early 1970s. The United States has had the highest incarceration rate in the world for well over a decade (Western 2006; Uggen, Manza, and Thompson 2006; Glaze and Bonczar 2009). Today, the United States incarcerates a larger percentage of its population than at any point in its history. Currently, about 502 people per 100,000 are held in United States prisons (USDOJ 2010; figure 1.1). When we add in the jail population, the number rises to 756 people per 100,000 (Walmsley 2008). Figure 1.2 shows the incarceration rates of the major Western democracies. The American incarceration rate is five times larger than England's (153 per 100,000), six times larger than Australia's (129 per 100,000), more than ten times the rate of Sweden (74 per 100,000), and more than twelve times that of Japan (63 per 100,000) (Walmsley 2008). By any definition or comparison, then, the United States is exceptional with respect to its incarceration rate.[8]

While most observers focus on the volume of American inmates, the racial disparity in the likelihood of imprisonment is both more striking and more consequential for social inequality. For black men born since the late 1960s, the risk of having been imprisoned by their early thirties was about one in four (Pettit and

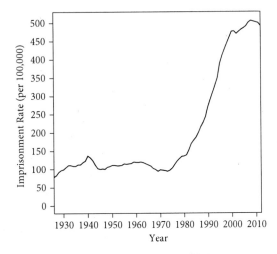

FIGURE 1.1 American Imprisonment Rate, 1925–2011

Source: Bureau of Justice Statistics "Prisoners in the United States" Series

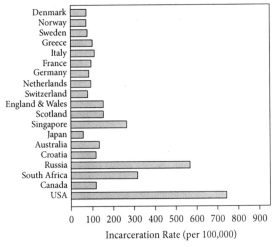

FIGURE 1.2 Incarceration Rates by Nation, 2008–2011

Source: World Prison List (world figures)

Western 2004; Western and Wildeman 2009), greater than their chance of completing college. For black men who did not complete high school, the risk of having experienced imprisonment by their early thirties ranged from 60 percent to 70 percent (Western and Wildeman 2009; Pettit and Western 2004). The risk for white men—even those who did not complete high school—was much lower (at 11 percent; Pettit and Western 2004). These risks were especially pronounced in the most disadvantaged neighborhoods, where even more individuals experienced incarceration (Clear 2007; Sampson and Loeffler 2010).

Mass Imprisonment and Mass Reductions in Crime?

Before assessing the consequences of the sea change in imprisonment for inequality, we must first consider how the shift has affected public safety. On the most basic level, one cannot ignore that the United States has enjoyed unprecedented declines in the crime rate over the four decades since the prison boom took off. This potentially suggests large benefits of the prison boom for public safety. Indeed, a cursory examination of national patterns in crime and incarceration over the last four decades would lead any reasonable person to conclude that the prison boom reduced crime (Bureau of Justice Statistics 2011). Yet a cursory look might also cause one to overestimate the effects of incarceration on crime (Durlauf and Nagin 2011; Wakefield and Uggen 2010). High incarceration states, for example, did not enjoy much larger declines in crime than did low incarceration states. Several other factors also decreased the crime rate, among them economic expansions, advances in policing, and shifts in the age structure of the population, to name but a few.

In the presence of a number of alternative and co-occurring explanations, the direct effect of imprisonment on crime is exceedingly difficult to calculate, and so the range of estimates produced by social scientists is large. The best evidence suggests that increases in the incarceration rate reduced the violent crime rate by as little as 10 percent and as much as 30 percent (Wakefield and Uggen 2010). Even the low estimate, 10 percent, is large by social scientific standards and ought not be taken lightly. That said, research on the crime-reducing benefits of incarceration tends to focus on estimating *average* effects of incarceration on crime over a long period—between the late 1970s and early 1990s (Levitt 1996), for instance. If the profiles of the average individual held in prisons and jails in 1970 and in 2010 were similar, this method would be appropriate. Yet we know that individuals who are incarcerated today differ greatly from those incarcerated in an earlier era. Indeed, prison sentences were once reserved for the most heinously violent or doggedly persistent criminals; however, those who have increasingly filled the cells during the prison boom represent far less danger to society. If an accurate portrait of an offender in 1970 is that of a violent recidivist, an accurate one today might be a petty offender who is struggling with drug or alcohol addiction.

This shift in the composition of the penal population is vital for our understanding of the costs and benefits of mass imprisonment. It suggests that the crime-fighting benefits of imprisonment should have decreased dramatically as those who filled the cells were less likely to be violent and to be recidivists. Although research testing this hypothesis is sparse, one article suggests that this is precisely what occurred. Rucker Johnson and Steven Raphael (2012) show that the decline in the violent crime rate associated with a 1 percent increase in the imprisonment rate has diminished from about .79 (1978–1990) to .21 (1991–2004) for violent crime and .43 (1991–2004) to .25 (1991–2004) for property crime. Although their analysis supports the high estimate of the crime-fighting benefits of imprisonment demonstrated by Steven Levitt (1996) for the early period, the results for the post-1990 period suggest that the imprisonment-crime relationship is now weak enough that imprisonment's consequences for inequality may now be more important than its consequences for crime (see also Western 2006).

Mass Imprisonment and Inequality

Based on these new findings, it is clear that we cannot evaluate mass incarceration only with respect to reductions in crime. As the prison population has exploded, social scientists have documented a variety of consequences that must be weighed against incarceration's crime reduction benefits. One direction of research emphasizes how imprisonment distorts social statistics; another estimates the effects of imprisonment on adult men's life chances and on the life chances of the women and children tied to them.

If the benefits of mass incarceration are often overestimated, the costs of mass incarceration are more often described as "hidden." A growing inmate population, for example, causes us to underestimate the unemployment rate by removing large portions of the unemployed from our calculations—since prisoners cannot look for work, they cannot be counted among the unemployed (Western 2006). Similar processes play out with respect to the high school dropout rate and voter participation (Pettit 2012; Manza and Uggen 2006). The large prison population also gives the impression that racial disparities are improving when they are actually at best staying the same. To take but one example, the much-touted gains in racial disparities in earnings during the economic expansion of the 1990s were in fact nonexistent because the lowest wage earners among African Americans were increasingly drawn into the prison system, and not counted in official economic statistics (Western 2006).

Another branch of research estimates the long-term consequences of a spell in prison for inmates, their partners and children, and their communities. Among the most studied of these effects is the influence of mass imprisonment on racial disparities in earnings. A criminal record imposes a drop in earnings of about 10 percent to 30 percent (Western 2006), some of which is attributable to the stigma employers attach to a criminal record (Pager 2003). For men who are black, having spent time in prison produces a double disadvantage that is almost insurmountable in the labor market, with some evidence showing employer preferences for white males with a felony conviction over black males without one (Pager 2003). Incarceration relegates former inmates to low-paying, often temporary jobs (Raphael and Weiman 2007) and imposes long-term wage and earnings penalties (Geller, Garfinkel, and Western 2011; Pettit and Western 2004; Pettit and Lyons 2007; Western 2002; but see Kling 2006; Grogger 1995).

The financial costs of imprisonment are passed on to the partners of inmates as well (Braman 2004; Comfort 2008; Grinstead et al. 2001). In addition to reproducing the household labor of the incarcerated partner, maintaining a relationship is expensive. Visiting, sending packages and letters, and receiving collect phone calls, all necessary for keeping in touch with an incarcerated loved one, cost money. Legal debt imposes costs on inmates as well as their families, and nonpayment of these debts can result in a seizure of assets, including homes (Harris, Evans, and Beckett 2010: 1788–1789). Incarceration also has the effect of piling disadvantage on vulnerable families, delivering a "serious and sometimes lethal blow to an already weakened family structure" (Hagan and Coleman 2001: 354). Incarceration affects family structure by breaking up intact families (Comfort 2007), which is harmful for the roughly half of children living with their father prior to his incarceration, or by rendering those who have been incarcerated unattractive on the marriage market (Edin 2000; Lopoo and Western 2005).

The research, then, demonstrates substantial individual-level effects of imprisonment; but the magnitude of the effects of the prison boom on inequality is bounded by the distribution from which inmates are drawn (Wildeman and Muller 2012). Because men who experience incarceration would have been unlikely to earn much regardless, the implications of imprisonment for inequality in lifetime earnings are bound to be small—even in the face of large individual-level effects. One analysis, for example, shows that the black-white gap in lifetime earnings would be only 3 percent smaller absent increases in imprisonment (Western

2006), suggesting that the majority of the racial gap in lifetime earnings among men remains unexplained after considering changes in incarceration. Other analyses, moreover, find that the labor market effects of imprisonment are not driven by the length of the sentence, beyond the earnings lost during the period of incarceration (Kling 2006). The prison boom is implicated in the somewhat larger racial disparities in the health (Massoglia 2008; Schnittker and John 2007), civic engagement (Manza and Uggen 2006), and marriage rates (Western and Wildeman 2009) of adult men, and in each case, incarceration imposes harm. Yet, because of the disadvantages these men already face, the consequences of mass imprisonment for inequalities among adult men in each of these domains may be much smaller than originally suspected.

CHILDREN OF THE PRISON BOOM: MASS INCARCERATION AND THE FUTURE OF INEQUALITY

If mass imprisonment's effects on inequality among adult men are small, then how could mass imprisonment shape the future of American inequality? We argue that a shift in emphasis from the consequences of mass imprisonment for inequality among adult men to inequality among their children reveals important, previously unacknowledged effects.

This shift makes sense because the incarceration of a parent touches a sufficiently large number of children to exert individual- and aggregate-level effects. More than 3 percent of American children (about 2.7 million) currently have a parent imprisoned (Western and Pettit 2010), and the number of children who have *ever* had a parent imprisoned is much higher (see chapter 2). To put this in perspective, consider that about one percent (or one million) American children will experience divorce this year (Cohen 2002). Another 3 percent will witness domestic violence (American Psychological Association 1996).

About 1 percent of American children are on the autism spectrum (Centers for Disease Control and Prevention 2010), and 6 percent are academically gifted (National Association for Gifted Children 2008). Consider the amount of research and discussion each of these groups receives (and merits). That the share of children of incarcerated parents is similar (or larger) in size suggests these children deserve far more attention than they currently receive.

We also advocate this shift because children's life chances are less fixed than those of their parents and much more amenable to intervention. Put simply, by the time most people enter prison, their life course is already largely determined. The same cannot be said for the children of prisoners, for whom the world is still very much open. Going to prison may have a small effect on inequality among adult men, whose life chances are so constrained, but it could have a much larger effect on inequality among children.

Plan of the Book

Through a series of empirical analyses, we demonstrate the substantial and devastating effects of paternal incarceration for children. In addition to detailing individual-level effects, we show that mass imprisonment contributes to racial disparities in several important determinants of child well-being. We identify the prison boom as a causal force behind current disparities in well-being and detail the social consequences yet to come.

For mass imprisonment to have intergenerational effects on inequality, it must do two things. First, it must disproportionately touch the lives of disadvantaged children. Based on the social patterning of the risk of imprisonment for adult men, we can expect that disadvantaged children are more likely to have a parent go to prison. Yet, although we know how many black and white children have a parent in prison on any given day, we have no idea how these daily risks accumulate over the course of a childhood. These are the questions chapter 2 seeks to answer: What is the cumulative risk of parental imprisonment for black and white children born in 1978 and 1990? And how do these risks vary by parental education? In answering these questions, we provide insight into how large the effects of the prison boom on inequality among children might be.

For mass imprisonment to exacerbate inequality among children, it must not only be common but also must meet a second condition: it must have negative consequences for the children caught in its web. Deciphering the channels through which parental imprisonment harms children is a difficult task—and it is one we undertake in chapter 3. Drawing on qualitative and quantitative data, we argue that although parental imprisonment helps some children, it harms far more children. This might seem a naïve claim. Parents who go to prison, after all, were criminally active and faced substantial obstacles as parents, including abuse and neglect in their own childhoods, spotty work histories, and drug and alcohol abuse, to name just a few. That said, inmates are parents, too, and affect their children in much the same way all parents do. We find substantial evidence, not only of high involvement among many inmate parents, but also of destructive effects of parental imprisonment on children across a variety of domains.

Theory and evidence do not always align, so we also need to test whether parental incarceration harms children as expected. This is the task we undertake in chapters 4, 5, and 6. In chapter 4, we estimate effects on children's behavioral and mental health problems using the two data sets best suited to the task—the Fragile Families and Child Wellbeing (FFCW) study and the Project on Human Development in Chicago Neighborhoods (PHDCN). We focus on these broad outcomes not only because most parents can remember a time when their children acted out or withdrew following a traumatic experience, but also because exhibiting these behaviors at high levels turns out to be a good predictor of problems in adolescence and adulthood, including teenage pregnancy, becoming a high school dropout, and criminal involvement. We find consistent evidence that the incarceration of a parent makes a bad situation worse for disadvantaged children, resulting in increases in internalizing, externalizing, and total behavioral problems, as well as substantial increases in physical aggression. Yet we also find that if the father was incarcerated for a violent crime or engaged in domestic violence, the harmful effects of paternal incarceration on children are less pronounced—to the point that there are sometimes even protective effects of paternal incarceration.

We turn our attention to infant mortality in chapter 5. Using the best data available—the Pregnancy Risk Assessment Monitoring System (PRAMS)—we estimate the effects of parental incarceration on the risk of infant death. The incarceration of a parent, often but not always a father, is associated with a substantial and statistically significant increase in the risk of infant mortality. Consistent with our findings from chapter 4, these effects are concentrated among infants whose fathers had not recently engaged in domestic violence toward the mother. Parental incarceration imposes no significant additional risks for infants with fathers who had been abusive recently.

In chapter 6, we examine the effects of paternal incarceration on child homelessness. By considering catastrophic events like infant mortality and homelessness—both of which have substantial black-white disparities in the risk of experiencing them—we show how mass parental imprisonment affects not only common outcomes, such as acting out or withdrawing, but also those that are far less common but far more serious. As was the case in the previous two chapters, we find consistent evidence that the incarceration of a father is associated with a substantial increase in the risk of child homelessness. One important difference, however, is that we find clear evidence that the negative effects of paternal incarceration on the risk of homelessness are concentrated among black children, suggesting that mass imprisonment may have played an especially pronounced role in increasing disparities in child homelessness.

Since our end goal is to estimate effects on social inequality—not individual children—in chapter 7 we estimate the effects of changes in the risk of parental imprisonment on racial inequalities in children's behavioral and mental health problems, infant mortality rates, and risks of homelessness. We find that mass imprisonment has done much more to exacerbate inequalities among children than among adult men. Estimates for adult men, most notably in earnings, hover around 3 percent (Western 2006); we find that mass imprisonment exacerbated black-white inequalities in children's externalizing behavioral problems by 14 percent to 26 percent, internalizing behavioral problems by 25 percent to 46 percent, and infant mortality rates by 9 percent to 18 percent. We find even more substantial effects on black-white disparities in child homelessness, which is partly a function of the fact that effects of paternal incarceration on black children's risk of being homeless were substantial, whereas the effects for whites were small. Indeed, our results suggest that the majority of the increase in black-white disparities in child homelessness were likely driven by mass imprisonment. Taken together, the results of our work show that the effects of mass incarceration on childhood inequality are too large to ignore.

In chapter 8, we conclude by discussing what our findings suggest about how imprisonment will shape the future of American inequality. We close by discussing a few policy solutions that have the potential to substantially ameliorate the consequences of mass imprisonment for future generations of children. Even though we have yet to feel the full weight of the consequences of mass imprisonment for social inequality, there are some key policy solutions we can pursue to ensure that mass imprisonment will not continue to shape inequalities beyond the next generation.

Mass incarceration is implicated in a host of racial disparities across a number of domains, and scholars of the modern prison describe it as a common experience for marginalized men. The unique contribution of our work is to expand the literature by bringing the children of incarcerated parents into the conversation. We start by showing that parental incarceration is heartbreakingly common for marginalized children. We then show that, even for kids at high risk of problems, parental incarceration makes a bad situation worse. We then show harmful effects of parental incarceration on mental health and behavioral problems, infant mortality, and homelessness. Contrary to a great deal of other research on the consequences of mass incarceration for inequality, these harms translate into large-scale increases in racial inequalities at the aggregate level. Taken together, we demonstrate current racial disparities in child well-being that are a direct result of parental incarceration and link the inequalities of today to the disparities of tomorrow.

Michael and Nathaniel Revisited

An unrelenting prison boom marked by racial disparities in imprisonment, characterized the last third of the twentieth century. There are mounting indications today, however, that high incarceration states have topped out; some states are reducing prison populations for the first time in decades. Consider California, which has long been a poster child for high incarceration rates and tough sentencing laws (Barker 2009; Page 2011; Simon 2007). The state is currently under federal order to reduce its prison population by 30,000 inmates and recently moved thousands of inmates to non-revocable parole to prevent re-incarcerations. This shift suggests that the American imprisonment rate could be substantially lower in the not-too-distant future and that reaching that goal may not result in a new crime epidemic.

Yet, we caution against too much optimism because of the damaging consequences of mass imprisonment for the children of the prison boom. We began this chapter by contrasting the experiences of Michael and Nathaniel, who each experienced paternal incarceration during childhood and went on to lead vastly different young lives. Michael's story, like the recent reductions in imprisonment, suggests a certain level of optimism because it shows the resilience of some children. Nathaniel's story, however, like the vast majority of cases, shows that the American experiment in mass imprisonment has left literally millions of children, many of them African American, far worse off than they were. Optimism about reductions in the imprisonment rate and the resilience of children must therefore be set against the backdrop of the children of the prison boom—a lost generation now coming of age.

THE SOCIAL PATTERNING OF

PARENTAL IMPRISONMENT

OUR GOAL IS to consider the long-term implications of mass imprisonment for American inequality by showing how it affects childhood inequality. For any event to influence inequality, it must be (1) common, (2) unequally distributed, and (3) result in negative outcomes. Absent the first two conditions, any social phenomenon that touches the lives of children, even if very harmful to child well-being or extremely traumatic, is unlikely to have large effects on childhood inequality.

Large-scale changes in the business cycle provide a useful corollary. Consistent with other downturns, the effects of the Great Recession, for example, on the black unemployment rate far surpassed those on the white employment rate (Couch and Fairlie 2010). By mid-2011, the white unemployment rate was about 8 percent, whereas the black umeployment rate was 16.7 percent (Bureau of Labor Statistics 2011), a dramatic increase in inequality since the period immediately preceding the Great Recession. Beyond effects on unemployment, the downturn resulted in a retrenchment of black-white wealth disparities. In 2009, the black-white wealth disparity in median households had increased to over twenty to one, the highest disparity in quite some time (Kochhar, Fry, and Taylor 2011). Given the many studies showing that parental unemployment and familial wealth shape child well-being and the increase in racial inequalities in unemployment and wealth caused by the Great Recession, this economic shift might lead to increases in racial inequality among children that extend into the future. It is possible that another large-scale shift— that of the mass incarceration of millions of African American fathers—could increase racial inequality in child well-being in the same way.

Although traumatic events like the mass unemployment of parents may contribute to increasing social inequality, it does not then follow that all traumatic events contribute to increasing social inequality. Contrast the influence of widespread unemployment on racial inequality with the aggregate-level effects of foster care placement. Whether being in foster care is better or worse for children than being with their families is hotly debated (Bartholet 1999, 2000; Guggenheim 2000); yet the most stringent tests suggest that being in the foster care system is worse for children, on average, than remaining in their home of origin (Doyle Jr. 2007, 2008). This may seem surprising because before a child enters foster care, both parents are generally absent from the household or struggling with problems of their own (such as addiction) and/or engaging in damaging behaviors (such as abuse). Yet the periodic loss of a parent and the consistent moves between households that come with foster care placement appear to trump the often-damaging behaviors of parents. So, since foster care is, on average, harmful to development, and if foster care placement is common and unequally distributed, then it may have important effects on childhood inequality. Foster care *is* unequally distributed; black children are 3.8 times more likely to be in foster care than white children (US Department of Health and Human Services 2009).[1] Yet, few children likely *ever* experience this event—although no estimates of the share of children who ever do have yet to be calculated.

Only 1.1 percent of black children and a scant .3 percent of white children are in foster care on any given day (US Department of Health and Human Services 2009).[2] With such low point-in-time risks, it is unlikely that enough children experience foster care placement for it to have large effects on social inequality—devastating though it may well be in the lives of individual children.

To take a final example, consider maternal depression. The best evidence suggests that growing up with a depressed mother, like being placed in foster care, has negative effects on child well-being (Turney 2011; Cummings and Davis 1994). However, unlike for foster care placement (and the incarceration of a parent), few would argue that having a depressed mother is good for children. Given these negative effects, we might ask if maternal depression can affect inequality between black and white children. Maternal depression is sufficiently common to influence childhood inequality. About one in six Americans will ever experience a major depressive episode (MDD), the diagnostic term for what we often refer to as "depression," at some point in their lives, with women at highest risk (Kessler et al. 2003). Although MDD is sufficiently common to have large effects on childhood inequality, they are not unequally distributed across racial and ethnic groups to any great degree (Kessler et al. 2003; Williams et al. 2007). So, despite its high prevalence in the population, maternal depression is unlikely to have substantial effects on childhood inequality.

Neither foster care placement nor growing up with a depressed mother is likely to have substantial effects on childhood inequality despite the negative effects of both on individual children. In contrast, parental unemployment is common, racially disparate, and likely to negatively affect childhood well-being. Is parental imprisonment like foster care placement, parental depression, or parental unemployment? In this chapter, we begin our analysis of this question by considering whether parental imprisonment is both common and unequally distributed enough to influence national levels of childhood inequality if it has negative effects on children.

We start by showing how the daily risk of parental imprisonment and inequality in that risk has increased since the late 1970s. We close by documenting inequality in the risk of having a parent imprisoned over the duration of childhood. In so doing, we highlight parental imprisonment as a common experience for poor and minority children. As imprisonment has become a common stage in the life course for their fathers (Pettit and Western 2004; Western and Wildeman 2009), so has parental imprisonment become common for their children.

THE EMERGENCE OF PARENTAL IMPRISONMENT AS A CHILDHOOD RISK

The dramatic increase in the American imprisonment rate since the mid-1970s is well-known.[3] Yet, until recently, it was unclear how the number and proportion of children with a parent incarcerated on any given day had changed over time or how unequally distributed this risk is. This is unfortunate because without these estimates, it is difficult to ascertain whether parental incarceration is now common and unequally distributed enough to have effects on childhood inequality or whether, like other events such as foster care placement and maternal depression, it is not.

In figure 2.1, we present estimates of changes in the percentage of children with a parent incarcerated between 1980 and 2008. As will be our custom, we also present estimates for both blacks and whites since our focus is on black-white inequality. We confine our analysis to a comparison of black and white children for two reasons. First, the contrast in incarceration rates is starkest between blacks and whites; incarceration rates for Hispanics (and most other racial and ethnic groups) fall between the two. Second, as a practical matter, Hispanics are inconsistently classified in the historical incarceration data we use for our estimates, making it difficult to calculate the risk of parental incarceration for this group in the early years of the data. We anticipate that the results we discuss here would apply in much the same direction (if not magnitude) to Hispanic children.

Unlike the other results presented in this chapter, the emphasis in figure 2.1 is on parental *incarceration*, encompassing jail and prison incarceration, rather than parental *imprisonment*, which includes only prison incarceration. We focus more broadly on incarceration here to illustrate just how many children have a parent locked up on any given day, which presents a starker picture of how many children have a parent who is potentially absent from

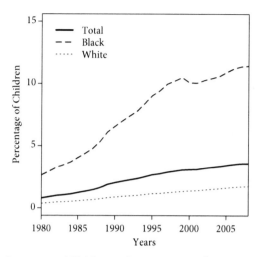

FIGURE 2.1 Percentage of Children with an Incarcerated Parent, 1980–2008
Source: Pettit, Western, and Sykes 2009

their life because of incarceration. In the remainder of the chapter, we focus solely on parental *imprisonment* because data on inmates in local jails do not contain all the information we need to estimate how many children will experience parental incarceration. Thus, the estimates we present later for the cumulative risk of parental imprisonment (perhaps dramatically) underestimate the percentage of children who will ever have a parent incarcerated.

Figure 2.1 shows the percentage of all American children with a parent incarcerated from 1980 to 2008, as well as showing how the percentages differ for black children and white children. On the most basic level, these estimates show that having a parent incarcerated is common. In 1980, about .80 percent of children could expect to have a parent incarcerated on any given day—a number that falls not too far from what we noted earlier for the percentage of children in foster care on any given day. Yet by 2008, this risk had increased dramatically to about 3.58 percent of all American children. Thus, between 1980 and 2008, the number of children with a parent incarcerated on any given day increased from roughly 1 in 120 to about 1 in 28. Parental incarceration is now fairly common for American children.

Perhaps more importantly, however, these estimates also highlight that parental imprisonment is not only common but also unequally distributed with respect to race. According to the estimates, the daily risk of parental incarceration for black children is 11.42 percent by 2008, a far cry not only from the 1.75 percent of white children who can expect to have a parent incarcerated in 2008 but also from the 2.65 percent of black children with a parent incarcerated in 1980. Although the risk has stabilized in recent years, the profound growth of the risk of parental imprisonment through the 1990s is noteworthy, as it highlights that parental incarceration has been common for black children for some time. The long-standing influence of race is also quite transparent in figure 2.1, as a substantially larger percentage of black children had a parent incarcerated in 1980 (2.65 percent) than white children did in 2008 (1.75 percent).

Figure 2.1 suggests that parental incarceration is common and unequally distributed. Yet even these estimates are a dramatic *underestimate* of the black-white difference in the risk of having an incarcerated parent. So while the 9.67 percent difference in 2008 between black children and white children—11.42 percent versus 1.75 percent—is substantial, the difference in ever experiencing this event is sure to be far greater. The estimates we now present reveal that the implications of mass imprisonment for future inequality are far worse than these point-in-time estimates suggest.

FROM DAILY RISKS TO CUMULATIVE RISKS

Children's risk of parental imprisonment, like the lifetime risk of imprisonment for adult men, accumulates over time, so it is unlikely that *only* 11.42 percent of black children can expect to ever have a parent imprisoned. To consider this possibility, we ask not what the daily risk of parental imprisonment is, but what a child's risk of *ever* having a parent imprisoned is and how this risk has changed over time. The next section calculates the cumulative risk of parental imprisonment, estimating the risk of parental imprisonment by the age of fourteen and comparing this risk across two birth cohorts (1978 and 1990), race (black and white), parent's sex (fathers and mothers), and parent's level of educational attainment (less than a high school degree, only a high school degree, and some college education). By providing these new estimates, we describe how the risks of parental imprisonment have evolved since the onset of mass imprisonment, how much racial and class variation there is in these risks, and whether both paternal and maternal imprisonment could have important implications for childhood inequality.[4]

THE RISKS OF PATERNAL AND MATERNAL IMPRISONMENT

Figure 2.2 presents estimates of the cumulative risk of imprisonment of a father by age fourteen for black and white children born in 1978 and 1990. The risk of paternal imprisonment was small for white children born in 1978—about one in fifty—and grew modestly between 1978 and 1990 to just over one in thirty. Racial disparities in imprisonment are startling. Black children born in 1978 had a one in seven chance of having a father sent to prison by their fourteenth birthday, a risk far greater than the one in fifty for white children born in the same year. The growth in this risk is also notable, as one in four black children born in 1990 had their father imprisoned by age fourteen, roughly a doubling of this risk since the late 1970s. To return to our reasons for doing this exercise, consider that this leads to an absolute black-white difference in the cumulative risk of paternal imprisonment of 21.5 percent (25.1 percent for black children minus 3.6 percent for white children), which is far greater than the 9.67 percent black-white

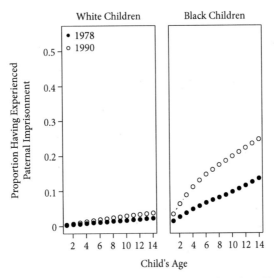

FIGURE 2.2 Cumulative Risk of Paternal Imprisonment for White Children and Black Children Born in 1978 and 1990

Source: Authors' calculation

difference found for the daily risk of parental incarceration in figure 2.1. Absolute disparity in these risks of paternal imprisonment is shocking, but the timing of these events is just as noteworthy. As figure 2.2 shows, black children are more likely to have their father imprisoned at any point before their *first* birthday than white children are to have their father imprisoned before their *fourteenth* birthday.

Given vast disparities in the incarceration rates of men and women, it is no great surprise that the risk of maternal imprisonment for children was far smaller than the risk of paternal imprisonment. In 1980, at the beginning of the prison boom, the incarceration rate of men was 275 per 100,000, compared to only 11 per 100,000 for women. Even today, well into the prison boom, incarceration rates are 954 per 100,000 for men and 68 per 100,000 for women (Sabol, West, and Cooper 2009). While it is the case

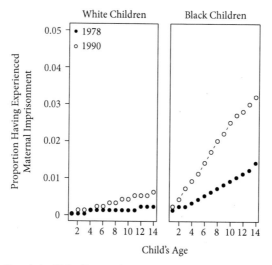

FIGURE 2.3 Cumulative Risk of Maternal Imprisonment for White Children and Black Children Born in 1978 and 1990, by Paternal Education

Source: Authors' calculation

that the dynamics of the prison boom greatly increased the imprisonment of women, incarceration continues to be largely a man's experience.

As figure 2.3 shows, the risk of maternal imprisonment for white children born in 1990 still barely exceeded 1 in 200. Even after the onset of the prison boom, the risk of maternal imprisonment for white children is negligible. The same cannot be said for black children. Although it is much smaller than the risk of paternal imprisonment, the risk of maternal imprisonment for black children born in 1990 was about one in thirty (3.3 percent), 135 percent greater than the risk experienced by children born in 1978. To put this in context, consider that the risk of maternal imprisonment for black children (3.3 percent) is nearly the same as the risk of paternal imprisonment for white children (3.6 percent). Though few black children will experience their mother going to prison at any point in their childhood, their risk of experiencing it is far from small and, like paternal imprisonment, much larger than the risk for white children.

CLASS DISPARITIES IN THE RISKS OF PATERNAL AND MATERNAL IMPRISONMENT

Estimates of the risk of parental imprisonment for black children and for white children underscore racial inequality, but they cannot shed light on class inequality. To provide insight into how class also shapes the risk of parental imprisonment, we present estimates of the risks of paternal imprisonment and maternal imprisonment for black children and white children whose parents dropped out of high school, completed high school only, or attended college. It is possible, for example, that racial differences in parental imprisonment merely reflect racial differences in resources and education, a common cause of crime (Arum and LaFree 2008).

An examination of figure 2.4 suggests that racial differences in educational attainment cannot explain large racial disparities in parental imprisonment. While both black children and white children of low-education parents are at greater risk of parental imprisonment, the risk is much more pronounced for black children. As figure 2.4 highlights, the risk of paternal imprisonment is small for white children born in 1978 regardless of paternal education. White children of high school dropouts had a one in twenty-five chance of their father being sent to prison. The risk shrinks to one in fifty for white children of high-school-educated fathers, and one in seventy for white children of college-educated fathers. Among white children, risks of paternal imprisonment grew the most for those with non-college-educated fathers. Although growth in the risk of paternal imprisonment was notable for white children of high school dropouts—up from 4.1 to 7.2 percent— growth was stronger for white children of high school graduates, more than doubling from 2.0 to 4.8 percent. For white children of

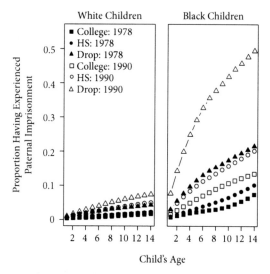

FIGURE 2.4 Cumulative Risk of Experiencing Paternal Imprisonment for White Children and Black Children Born in 1978 and 1990, by Paternal Education
Source: Authors' calculation

college-educated fathers, the risk of paternal imprisonment grew only 0.2 percentage points, from 0.9 percent to 1.1 percent. In fact, growth in the risk of paternal imprisonment for white children of college-educated fathers was so sparse that it is only when the risks of paternal imprisonment are magnified in figure 2.5 (by changing the y-axis) that any change in this risk becomes discernible to the naked eye. Class inequality in the risk of paternal imprisonment grew for white children; white children of college-educated parents experienced only a minimal increase in the risk of paternal imprisonment, while all other white children experienced large increases.

Class inequality in the risk of paternal imprisonment was also large for black children, as figure 2.4 highlights. Black children born to high school dropouts in 1978—before the prison boom had peaked—had a 22 percent chance of experiencing

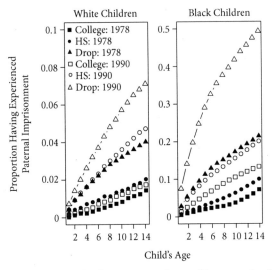

FIGURE 2.5 Cumulative Risk of Experiencing Paternal Incarceration for White Children and Black Children Born in 1978 and 1990, by Paternal Education

Source: Authors' calculation

paternal imprisonment; about one in ten black children of high school graduates and one in fourteen black children of college-educated parents experienced paternal imprisonment. The disadvantage of black children born in 1990 was even more pronounced. Over half (50.5 percent) of black children born in 1990 to high school dropouts had their father imprisoned, up 130 percent since 1978. Just as imprisonment has become a modal event in the life course of black men with low levels of educational attainment (Western and Wildeman 2009; Pettit and Western 2004), so too has paternal imprisonment become modal for their children. Even black children of highly educated parents are not fully insulated from the risk of paternal imprisonment, however. About 13 percent of black children of college-educated parents had a parent sent to prison. Although this risk is dwarfed by the risk for black children of high school dropouts, it is much larger than the risk for comparable white children. In fact, the risk of paternal imprisonment for black children of college-educated fathers (13.8 percent) is nearly twice the risk of paternal imprisonment for white children of high school dropouts (7.2 percent), again suggesting that racial disparities in the risk of parental imprisonment may trump other stratifying factors such as social class.

Figure 2.6 presents risks of maternal imprisonment that were much more modest than risks of paternal imprisonment but still show important variations by race. Whites born in 1978 and 1990 had a small risk of maternal imprisonment. The risk of maternal imprisonment for white children born in 1978 to high school dropouts was 1 in 500. By 1990, it had grown to 1 in 100. Although this rate of growth is large, white children of low-education mothers continue to have little risk of maternal imprisonment. White

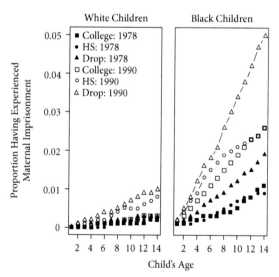

FIGURE 2.6 Cumulative Risk of Experiencing Maternal Incarceration for White Children and Black Children Born in 1978 and 1990, by Maternal Education

Source: Authors' calculation

children of college-educated mothers had even lower risks: about 1 in 300 of them had a mother imprisoned. The risk of maternal imprisonment is negligible for white children regardless of maternal education—even in the post-prison-boom birth cohort.

This is not the case for black children. For black children born in 1978, the risk of maternal imprisonment ranges from 1 in 100 to 1 in 50 depending on maternal education, a small but noteworthy risk of experiencing this event. By 1990, the risk of maternal imprisonment had increased substantially. For black children of high school dropouts, the risk of maternal imprisonment was 5 percent; the risk was 1 in 40 for black children of high school graduates. The rate of growth was larger for black children of low-education mothers than high-education mothers, although the risk for black children of college-educated mothers also grew. Again, comparing these risks to the risk of paternal imprisonment among white children is instructive. The risk of maternal imprisonment for black children born in 1990 whose mothers did not complete high school (5 percent) is higher than the risk of paternal imprisonment for white children born in 1990 to fathers who completed only high school (4.8 percent), suggesting that maternal imprisonment is as important a part of the childhood social experience for poor black children as paternal imprisonment is for white working-class children.

CONCLUSION

The results described in this chapter highlight the historical novelty of the risk of paternal imprisonment and, albeit to a lesser degree, that of maternal imprisonment faced by contemporary African American children. Prior to the prison boom, imprisonment was a rare punishment reserved only for the most heinous, persistent, or unlucky offenders. As such, the criminal justice system paid little attention to the children left behind when their fathers went to prison. Today, much has changed. For black children from the 1990 birth cohort—the twenty-two- and twenty-three-year-olds of today like Michael and Nathaniel—the risk of having a father imprisoned before their fourteenth birthday was one in four. For comparable white children, the risk was only about one in thirty. This massive absolute and relative disparity suggests that unlike other severe disadvantages such as foster care placement, parental imprisonment is now sufficiently common and unequally distributed that it can increase childhood inequality, provided it does children substantial harm.

The results speak not only to childhood inequality, however. Indeed, they speak to the unique risks faced by African American children. For instance, the risk of paternal imprisonment (25 percent) is only slightly lower than the probability of having a father who attended college (27 percent) for black children, and their risk of having an imprisoned father far exceeds the risk of MDD for the population (16 percent; Kessler et al. 2003). Considering the risks of paternal imprisonment for black children whose fathers did not complete high school paints a bleaker picture still, as the risk of paternal imprisonment for these children exceeds one in two. It is more likely for black children of low-education fathers to experience paternal imprisonment than not. For white children of high school dropout fathers, the risk was only 7 percent.

The risk of maternal imprisonment is also noteworthy. For white children it never exceeds 1 percent regardless of maternal education, but for all black children it is about 3.3 percent. This risk is noteworthy not just because it suggests that about one in thirty black children will ever have their mother imprisoned, but also because it is only slightly lower than the risk of paternal imprisonment for white children (3.6 percent). The rapid increases in the risk of maternal imprisonment for black children also provide a stark illustration of why about 30 percent of the massive increase in the number of foster care caseloads between 1985 and 2000 could have been due to changes in the female imprisonment rate (Swann and Sylvester 2006). Although we focus mostly on paternal rather than maternal imprisonment in this book (for reasons we discuss later), changes in the risk of maternal imprisonment had the potential to increase the risk of experiencing other severe forms of childhood disadvantage (such as foster care placement).

Changes in the risk of parental imprisonment and the concentration of these risks among black children are consequential for childhood inequality only if parental imprisonment is common, unequally distributed, and *has negative effects on children*. In the chapters to come, we continue to consider whether paternal incarceration helps, hurts, or has no effect on children.

BEFORE AND AFTER IMPRISONMENT

> He's a good dad, he did spend a lot of time with the kids
> [before he went to prison]...He's a great guy.
>
> —MICHELLE, *Mother of two*

> I know that he was a crook.
>
> —LUKE, *Son of incarcerated father*

> I took parenting classes, anger management, critical thinking,
> I went to barber school, victim impact classes. I did every-
> thing I could do [while in prison].
>
> —TERENCE, *Formerly incarcerated father*

> Both of them [biological mother and father] were crackheads
> and alcoholics. My biological mom, all of her sons and daugh-
> ters were in foster homes or her family understood that she
> couldn't take care of 'em.
>
> —NATHANIEL, *Son of incarcerated mother and incarcerated father*

THE COMMENTS OF Michelle, Luke, Terence, and Jacob, which
are taken from interviews with children and their caregivers completed during a longitudinal study of children of incarcerated
parents, simultaneously challenge and support our assertion that
paternal incarceration can harm children. On the one hand, we
have the "good dad" whose absence undoubtedly does his partner and children harm. On the other, we have the "crook" and the
"crackhead" whose absence likely affected his children little—and
maybe even helped them in some ways.

In this chapter, we use qualitative data on the home lives of the families of inmates before and after a parent's incarceration and quantitative data from a representative survey to ascertain whether the absence of the average incarcerated man helps, hinders, or has no effect on his family. Is the modal incarcerated father a crook, crackhead, or a great guy? These characterizations are too simplistic, but they do accurately represent the heterogeneity of today's prison population. The challenge for our analysis throughout the book is to separate the crooks from the merely imperfect fathers in order to estimate the effect of paternal incarceration for the average child.

Most people who end up in prison have serious problems and face significant disadvantages—they may be impulsive or dishonest ("a crook"), struggle with serious alcohol and drug addiction ("crackheads and alcoholics"), or attempt to do their best parenting under trying circumstances ("I did everything I could do"). The risk of parental imprisonment is unequally distributed not only by race and educational attainment, as we showed in chapter 2, but also by paternal characteristics, such as poor impulse control, mental health problems, and drug and alcohol addiction (Giordano 2010; Gottfredson and Hirschi 1990; Sampson 2011), as well as on other structural features, such as neighborhood disadvantage (Clear 2007; Sampson and Loeffler 2010).

The fact that these personal problems and structural disadvantages usually pre-date incarceration is relevant for two reasons. First, it implies that if the incarceration of a parent does harm children, the implications of mass imprisonment for future social inequality could be substantial indeed. After all, if children of imprisoned parents are disproportionately poor, African American, and residents of the most disadvantaged neighborhoods and also have parents who face mental health, addiction, or impulse-control problems, then mass imprisonment could further marginalize children already on the borders of society. The distribution of these characteristics is important because it suggests that the effects of mass imprisonment on the future of American inequality could be large—provided parental imprisonment harms children.

Yet the deep disadvantages the children of imprisoned parents face, even before their parent is taken to prison, presents both an empirical and a theoretical challenge for our analysis. The empirical issue centers around an interpretation fallacy that social scientists commonly refer to as "spuriousness"—the idea that the relationship between paternal incarceration and some outcomes (mental health and behavioral problems, infant mortality, or homelessness, for example) is not "real," and that both, in fact, result from some other (often unmeasured) common cause (poverty, for example). The spuriousness argument is certainly compelling in this context. Given the many other structural constraints children of the prison boom face on account of their neighborhoods of origin, race, class, and the parenting behaviors they are exposed to, we should expect them to fare worse than other children on a host of outcomes, even if their parent had never been imprisoned. Put simply, because disadvantage increases the likelihood of both paternal imprisonment *and* childhood mental health and behavioral problems, infant mortality, and homelessness, paternal imprisonment may not be a "true" cause of these problems.

The theoretical issue is similarly challenging. There are equally compelling arguments suggesting that paternal incarceration is harmful, beneficial, or has no effect on children. We argue that the average child is harmed by the experience, but this is certainly not universally true, an important point to recognize, especially in a book that mostly focuses on the "average effects" of paternal incarceration. As noted earlier, given the damaging behaviors their parents may have engaged in because of their own personal problems, the removal of their parent may actually make it easier for some children to thrive.

To ascertain the relationship of paternal incarceration to social inequality, we must estimate the effect of paternal incarceration on the average child. This requires that we distinguish among competing theories on the direction of paternal incarceration effects *and* attend to the spuriousness problem. In the end, we show that paternal incarceration is, on average, harmful for children and that the counterarguments suffer from four basic problems.

First, while many may assume that incarcerated parents are by definition bad parents, there is ample evidence to refute this. The pool of incarcerated parents is much more complex (as we highlight in the qualitative data in this chapter), and includes involved parents, abusive parents, and many that fall somewhere in between.

Second, the assumption that the loss of a parent to prison would be good—or at least not bad—for children suffers from the use of an erroneous comparison group. While it makes good sense to minimize the destructive influence of a parent's drug use or emotional instability, it does not follow that the complete loss of the parent will result in better outcomes for children. We show in this chapter that even parents who are inconsistently involved with their children may still represent a net gain for them.

Third, a parent's spell of incarceration has cascading effects, influencing family finances, relationships between children and the caregiver left behind, and a host of other difficulties. These effects are also not restricted to children who had a high-quality relationship with their father before he was incarcerated, which is especially relevant for the analysis to follow. Stress at home, financial instability, and stigma resulting from paternal incarceration affect all children, not merely those who lose an involved parent.

Finally, the characteristics of the pool of offenders in prison partially determine the effects of paternal incarceration on children, a point we illustrate in chapter 4 as well. As we pointed out in the introduction, the average inmate today is less likely to be a violent offender than in prior eras. The contemporary prison, then, may be more likely to house inconsistent or irresponsible parents but perhaps less likely to house harmful ones.

THE SOCIAL SITUATION OF CHILDREN BEFORE PARENTAL IMPRISONMENT

To consider how paternal incarceration affects children, we rely on quantitative data from the Fragile Families and Child Wellbeing (FFCW) study. These data are described in detail in the next chapter. For now, the key thing to note is that we draw on these data because they include extensive information on the family lives of a large sample of high-risk children who did and did not experience paternal incarceration.

We also utilize longitudinal qualitative data on a small sample of children and families who experienced the incarceration of a father (and, in one case, a mother as well).[1] These data, collected between 2004 and 2006, draw on the experiences of eight primary caregivers and fourteen children who completed all four possible interviews during the data collection period.[2] We use these data as case studies to add texture to the characteristics detailed in the FFCW analysis. Our snapshots of the children of the incarcerated are by no means representative, but they do provide illustrative cases to aid our thinking about family conditions prior to and following paternal incarceration. Table A2 in the methodological appendix describes the families in more detail.

We also use both data sets to examine *changes* in family life as a result of paternal incarceration and to assess whether parental incarceration made a bad situation better, worse, or had no effect on it. Using the FFCW survey, we start by comparing the situations of three-year-old children and their families who will and will not experience paternal incarceration at some point in the next two years. We break these comparisons up into (1) demographic traits of mothers and fathers, (2) characteristics of the household, and (3) characteristics of the father. In so doing, we provide a portrait of what the outcomes of these children would likely have been even if their fathers not had been incarcerated.

We focus on these characteristics because a large literature in child development suggests that each of these features shapes child well-being.

Differences in Demographic Traits

It will surprise few to learn that parental employment, socioeconomic status, and educational attainment have strong effects on children (see McLanahan and Percheski 2008; Breen and Jonsson 2005; Lichter 1997; Nelson 2004 for authoritative reviews). Children who grow up in poverty are more likely to be poor as adults, and parents who dropped out of high school or are unemployed have more difficulty raising their children. Since maternal race, education, and age significantly shape child well-being in a host of domains (McLeod and Nonnemaker 2000; McLanahan and Sandefur 1994; McLanahan and Percheski 2008; Entwisle and Alexander 1993; Grusky, Ku, and Szelényi 2008), these broad intergenerational processes suggest that their children would have been worse off than others even in the absence of paternal incarceration, assuming they are more disadvantaged on each of these characteristics.

Figure 3.1 shows how the race, education, and age of parents who will and will not soon experience a bout of paternal incarceration differ. Mothers who will soon have the father of their child incarcerated are dramatically more likely to be African American (63.9 percent to 45.2 percent) than other women and are also slightly less likely to be Hispanic (19 percent to 27.5 percent) or white (14.5 percent to 23.3 percent). They are more likely to have dropped out of high school (36.6 percent to 26.1 percent), far less likely to have completed any college (37.4 percent to 49.2 percent), and are about three years younger, on average.

Differences in paternal race and age were comparable to differences for mothers. Fathers who will eventually experience incarceration are far more likely to be African American (67.0 percent

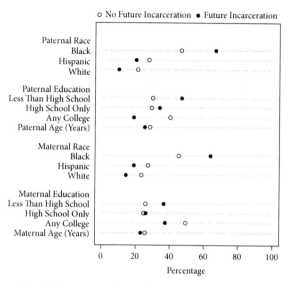

FIGURE 3.1 Race, Education, and Age of Fathers and Mothers by Future Paternal Incarceration

Source: Fragile Families & Child Wellbeing Study

to 46.8 percent) than white (10.1 percent to 21.1 percent) and about three years younger, on average, than men who will not soon experience incarceration. With respect to educational attainment, differences between men soon to experience incarceration and not soon to experience it are even more pronounced. Nearly half (46.9 percent) of men soon to experience incarceration had dropped out of high school, and less than one in five (19 percent) had attended college. For men who would not experience incarceration soon, only about 30 percent had dropped out of high school, and about two in five (40.5 percent) had completed some college. As with the mothers, descriptive statistics on the demographic traits of fathers who would eventually experience incarceration suggest that these children would have been at risk regardless.

Differences in Household Characteristics

The demographic characteristics highlighted in the FFCW data (and in chapter 2) extend to household characteristics. The incarcerated are more likely to be poor, have unstable romantic relationships, and have sporadic relationships with their children. Not surprisingly, each of these household characteristics—financial well-being (Duncan and Brooks-Gunn 1997; McLeod and Shanahan 1993), the relationship between the parents (Amato and Booth 2009), and the relationship between the father and the child—(Carlson and Magnuson 2011; but see King 1994) also shape child well-being. Similarly, family structure and father absence (McLanahan and Percheski 2008; McLanahan, Tach, and Schneider, forthcoming), family dissolution (Cherlin 1999), and household shifts (Cherlin and Chase-Lansdale 1998; Kiernan and Cherlin 1999; Fomby and Cherlin 2007) are linked to difficulty for children in several developmental domains, including socio-emotional development, mental health, and educational attainment.

In figure 3.2, we compare household characteristics of families soon to experience the incarceration of a father with those who will not experience paternal incarceration. As we would expect, the finances of households soon to have a father incarcerated were in grave disarray relative to those not about to experience that event. The income-to-poverty ratio, which is literally just the household income divided by the poverty line for a household of the same composition, for those households (1.1) was far lower than for other households (2.1), and the mother had also experienced more hardships, such as having her utilities turned off for being unable to pay her bills or being evicted for nonpayment of rent (1.2 to 0.8), recently. Given the importance of household finances and hardships for children (e.g., Duncan et al. 2011), these differences imply that the children of incarcerated parents were at high risk even before their father went to prison.

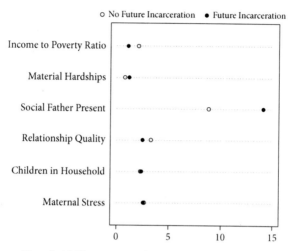

FIGURE 3.2 Household Characteristics by Future Paternal Incarceration
Source: Fragile Families & Child Wellbeing Study

Qualitative interviews with children of incarcerated parents show the same preincarceration problems. Of the families in the qualitative data, only one was doing well financially prior to the father's incarceration (and it is worth noting that the family's relative financial stability was driven by the father's drug selling). When asked about life before incarceration, financial difficulty was the modal response, among the others cited.

> Oh, our finances were horrible. We had two mortgages, we had every credit card maxed. We had, you know, but he had to have this and he had to have that. Our house was falling down around our ears.
>
> —SUSAN HARRISON, *Biological mother of two*

> A lot of financial stress. He was kinda trying to keep up with the Joneses; you gotta have all this stuff to show people. Regardless of what your money situation is like.
>
> —ALLISON FREEMAN, *Biological mother of two*

Perhaps most importantly, the children in every family interviewed were keenly aware of their family's economic difficulties (see also Nesmith and Ruhland 2008). In that regard, the experience of families with a parent incarcerated has much in common with the broader experience of disadvantaged families. Annette Lareau (2003), for example, points out that a major difference between poor and middle-class families is the extent to which financial matters are discussed in the presence of children—even when they are very young.

Figure 3.2 also shows the often substantial differences in the structure and quality of the relationship between their parents for children who are soon to experience the incarceration of a father and who are not soon to experience that event. Looking first at family structure, there were especially pronounced differences between families soon to experience incarceration and not soon to experience it in the percentage of parents who were married to each other (10.7 to 37.0 percent) as well as with no romantic relationship with one another (63.7 to 37.6 percent). The mothers of these children were also more likely to have a new romantic partner—a social father—residing with them (14.1 to 8.8 percent) and tended to report that their relationship to the soon to be inmate father was of significantly worse quality than were other women (3.3 to 2.5). Differences in other characteristics, such as the number of the mother's children in the household and the mother's parenting stress, were less pronounced. Again, given the well-documented relationship between the structure and quality of the relationship between the biological parents, these differences suggest that children of the incarcerated would be worse off regardless (Amato and Booth 2009; McLanahan and Percheski 2008).

Finally, figure 3.2 also shows large parenting differences between fathers soon to go to jail and not soon to go to jail. Mothers reported far lower levels of paternal shared responsibility (2.1 to 2.8) and cooperating in parenting (2.8 to 3.3), and somewhat lower levels of paternal engagement (4.9 to 5.0). Given the importance of the quality of paternal involvement for child well-being (Choi and Jackson 2011; Carlson and Magnuson 2011), this again suggests that the children of low-involvement fathers who are more likely to select into prison would have been doing worse even if their fathers hadn't been incarcerated. Still, incarceration is an important cause of reduced contact between father and child as well, and may result in added harm, even if the starting levels of contact are already low (Geller forthcoming).

In the qualitative data, there is substantial variation in the pre-incarceration involvement of fathers—some were wholly absent from the lives of their children, while others were engaged to the best of their abilities. The preincarceration fatherhood experiences of Jacob and Luke Anderson, for example, represent one extreme. Their father was sentenced to a lengthy prison term when his older son (Jacob) was a toddler and his younger son (Luke) was not yet born. Still, their father is a presence in their lives, whether as the "crook" Luke described at the beginning of the chapter or as the father Jacob hopes to know one day, suggesting possible differences by child's age at incarceration.

For other families, the preincarceration role played by the fathers was significant. To take one example, Michelle Johnson's ex-boyfriend received a twelve-year sentence for drug selling in 2000; nonetheless, in the quotation at the beginning of this chapter, she describes him as a "great father" and "a good friend." Despite having to travel a great distance, her children visit him several times a year, talk with him on the phone regularly, and eagerly await his release. Michelle also says of him:

> He's a good dad, he did spend a lot of time with the kids. Even now, he writes, writes them a lot and they do go see him whenever we can and, um, we send him cards and stuff, so he's a great guy.

Straddling these two extremes of disengagement and involvement are those who described the fathers of the children in their care as loving but inconsistently involved because of ongoing problems—often serious drug use. Martha Maxwell, for instance, adoptive mother and biological aunt of Nathaniel (and biological sister of Nathaniel's father), described the father-child relationship prior to incarceration as follows:

> No matter what he did, he still took the time to come by and see his son at least twice a month. I wouldn't let him take him anywhere because of his drug use, and I was afraid he would take him somewhere and not be safe and start using drugs and leave him with somebody to watch him. Which his mother has done in the past, so I just kind of…He's a good person if he can stay off of his drug.

Many of the children in the qualitative interviews described relatively good relationships with their fathers, and caregivers corroborated their descriptions. Children who were young when their father went to prison had a tendency to idealize him, as well. For example, Eric Johnson, at age nine, tells his interviewer that when his father is released, he and his father will move to Chicago; his sister Tanya, at age ten, says the family will all live together in their current home in Minnesota; and their mother, Michelle, however, reports in 2006 that she is no longer involved with their father romantically and has no plans to reside with him. Michelle is aware that her children's expectations are unrealistic:

> They want us to be back together. They still talk about what we was doing, sometimes they play games. They just say they wish he can come home. They say things like I'll be glad when my Dad get out so we can get a kitten. We have two!

Eric also says that if his Dad were out of prison, "everything would be easier." He believes the family would live in a better neighborhood and get a better-looking house. In the case of the Johnsons, it may be unclear how their father's incarceration has influenced their lives, but it is clear that he presents little danger to his children or to their mother.

Finally, the Howard family represents the clearest case of a flawed but good father who is removed from children who love him. Both mother and children describe Terence Howard as being involved and important to the family unit before his incarceration. Nina Howard worked hard to maintain her relationship with her husband while he was incarcerated, and the family struggled to remain connected. The Howard children describe his absence as a loss with lasting and wide-ranging consequences, highlighting stigma and missed school events, and describing his absence as a "hole" in their lives.

Overall, the FFCW and qualitative interviews highlight significant heterogeneity in preincarceration relationships between father, mother, and children. They also suggest that paternal involvement—as opposed to paternal characteristics—may not be the most important measure conditioning the effect of paternal incarceration on children. Some children had very little contact with their fathers but described incarceration as harmful, while others had a lot of contact with their fathers, and yet his incarceration appears to have been beneficial. We next turn to an analysis of the influence of paternal characteristics and their role in conditioning the effects of incarceration on children.

Differences in Paternal Characteristics

In figure 3.3, we address the possibility that some children might benefit from their father's incarceration by showing how fathers soon to be incarcerated and not compare on measures of impulsivity, domestic violence, and drug or alcohol abuse. Differences in impulsivity are not overwhelmingly large (2.3 to 2.1 percent), but they nonetheless exist. Differences in prior domestic violence against the mother (17.4 to 6.0 percent) and a history of drug or alcohol abuse (35.5 to 13.3 percent) are far more pronounced, and troublingly so. Are fathers with poor impulse control so bad for their children that their absence is a boon to child well-being? What about fathers who have engaged in domestic violence or

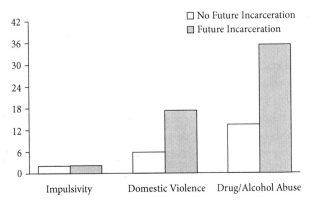

FIGURE 3.3 Paternal Impulsivity, Domestic Violence, and Drug/Alcohol Abuse by Future Paternal Incarceration

Source: Fragile Families & Child Wellbeing Study

have ongoing struggles with drug or alcohol addiction? Based on these differences, the removal of a father could enhance well-being for some children.

Contrast the Howard family, for example, with the Harrison and Freeman fathers. Both his wife and children describe Terence Howard, husband to Nina and father to her two children, as highly involved before his five-year prison term for drug selling and committed to parenthood during his incarceration.[3] The description offered by the Harrison and Freeman families could hardly be more different. Mr. Harrison and Mr. Freeman were both described as emotionally, physically, or sexually abusive to either their wives or children, and financial instability (worsened by incarceration but also present well before it) was a constant theme in the interviews with both families.

Mr. Harrison, married to Susan and father to two boys, was incarcerated for a series of violent sex offenses and re-incarcerated shortly after release for serious parole violations. In 2006, one year after her husband's release from his second incarceration, Susan described herself and her boys as in hiding, living in fear and "penny to penny," and continuing to pay for her ex-husband's sins. Similarly, Mr. Freeman was incarcerated for a violent sex offense and is described as abusive by his wife, and today his children express little desire to contact him. When asked to describe her family in an early interview, Kayla, the youngest child (at age thirteen), laughed and replied, "There's a book sitting on the counter called *The Sociopath Next Door*. I don't know anyone outside of my family who would pick up a book like that." During her last interview in 2006, Kayla expresses little attachment to her father and appears to have benefited from his incarceration, even though it worsened the family finances considerably.

The Harrison and Freeman experiences highlight the importance of paternal characteristics and the quality (rather than quantity) of paternal involvement. Both men were the rare cases in the qualitative data who were married to the mothers of their children, living in the home, and present in their children's lives prior to incarceration—all things that might suggest that paternal incarceration will impose harm. Although we might rate these men "high" on paternal involvement measures, the quality of that involvement was certainly quite low. From the standpoint of good parenting, the Harrison and Freeman fathers failed on every level, and their incarceration served as a respite from abuse. But this portrait of abuse was certainly not the norm, in either the qualitative interviews or the FFCW. For the other families interviewed, the modal description of the incarcerated father was of a flawed man, irresponsible and perhaps sometimes reckless, but not often dangerous. To briefly return to figure 3.3, this makes sense since 17.4 percent of soon-to-be-incarcerated fathers who had ever engaged in abuse means that fully 82.6 of incarcerated fathers—the vast majority—had not.

The Harrison and Freeman cases also show that paternal incarceration can have beneficial *as well as* harmful effects, even in the presence of abusive or otherwise terrible fathers. Of all those interviewed in the qualitative data, the Harrison and Freeman families, for example, experienced the largest shifts in economic well-being as a result of paternal incarceration. The Harrisons lost their home and acquired significant debt, and the Freemans were in arrears on their mortgage payments and facing foreclosure. We leave to future chapters the considerable work of teasing out whether these countervailing effects amount to a net benefit or harm for the average child, but these illustrative cases suggest caution for those who assume that the effects of paternal incarceration are, in any direction, uniform.

The obstacles presented by selection into incarceration are substantial as well. While we know that disadvantages weigh heavily on children during the transition to adulthood and that incarceration *signals* disadvantage, it is far more difficult to show that parental incarceration *causes* additional problems for children. Even before incarceration, as figures 3.2 and 3.3 suggest, the children of inmates had problems. The direction and strength of the relationship between paternal incarceration and outcomes for children also depends on the pool of incarcerated inmates. Are they more like Terence Howard or the Freeman and Harrison fathers? For many children, the incarceration of a parent makes a bad situation worse, but it may benefit others. It remains to seen whether the costs or benefits of paternal incarceration dominate for other families, who represent the majority of currently incarcerated inmates, although, as we argue in short order, the evidence points more toward negative effects than to null or positive ones.

MAKING A BAD SITUATION WORSE?

Quantitative Evidence

Given the obstacles children whose parents experience incarceration would have faced if their parents had not gone to prison, why would we expect paternal incarceration to harm children? Based on the disadvantages these children faced before they had a parent go to prison, we might expect null effects of parental incarceration. And based on the damaging behaviors their fathers engaged in, we might expect it to help them. The qualitative data show examples of both, as well as examples of harm. Yet the qualitative data give little sense of what the *average* effects of parental incarceration are. Therefore, we now turn to the quantitative data to show how *on average* the incarceration of a father makes a bad situation worse by disrupting the relationship between the parents and diminishing paternal involvement with children.

Using data from the FFCW study, figure 3.4 reports that the incarceration of a parent is associated with changes in the relationship between parents, paternal involvement, and paternal antisocial behaviors. Families experiencing paternal incarceration saw larger decreases in marriage (−3.9 percent to −0.1 percent), cohabitation (−7.5 percent to −6.5 percent), and being in a nonresidential relationship (−4.8 percent to −1.7 percent), leading to more substantial increases in being in no relationship with the mother (16.4 percent to 8.3 percent). Unsurprisingly, the shift toward being in no romantic relationship with the father was accompanied by larger increases in the share of mothers living with a new romantic partner (11.0 percent to 4.5 percent) and in low-quality relationships with the mother (.4 to .3), which might explain the greater decreases in paternal shared responsibility in parenting, cooperating in parenting, and engagement among fathers who had recently experienced incarceration (see also Geller Forthcoming).

Since children whose parents co-reside and are in a high-quality relationship do better on average than others, the introduction of a social father into the home may harm these children. And since children whose fathers are highly involved in their parenting also do better, these changes suggest that the incarceration of a father may have made a bad situation much worse for many of these children. Indeed, based on just the small list of important changes presented in figure 3.4, it would not be surprising if parental incarceration harmed children.

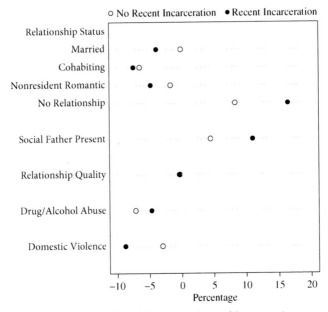

FIGURE 3.4 Change in Family Life by Recent Paternal Incarceration
Source: Fragile Families & Child Wellbeing Study

Yet, if the average effects of paternal incarceration on the social situations of children are negative, figure 3.4 also includes some indications that the incarceration of a father may improve the well-being of some children. Although children who experienced paternal incarceration did not experience larger declines in paternal drug or alcohol abuse than did other children (−4.7 percent to −7.2 percent), they did experience far greater declines in exposure to domestic violence (−8.8 percent to −3.0 percent), suggesting that for children who had been victims of (or witnesses to) domestic violence, the incarceration of a father might improve their well-being. Little research tests this possibility, but the alignment between the FFCW data and the qualitative interviews provides evidence that domestic violence may moderate the association between paternal incarceration and child well-being.

Qualitative Evidence

Existing research suggests that paternal incarceration compromises family functioning in a number of ways. The most well-researched consequence concerns family finances. We've shown here that economic struggle was common among children of the incarcerated prior to imprisonment in both the FFCW and the qualitative interviews. Yet incarceration is likely to impose additional strains. First, incarceration disproportionately draws in men with the poorest job prospects (Pettit and Western 2004), preventing them from contributing funds to family members during their incarceration and further diminishing their employability upon their release (Pager 2003; Western 2002, 2006). Second, incarceration is associated with elevated risks of marital dissolution (Apel et al. 2010; Lopoo and Western 2005; Massoglia, Remster, and King 2011). Since paternal financial contributions are shaped by earnings and by the father's relationship with the mother, incarceration diminishes paternal financial contributions (Geller, Garfinkel, and Western 2011). Third, the accumulation of legal debt as a result of incarceration disrupts familial finances "by reducing family income; by limiting access to opportunities and resources such as housing, credit, transportation, and employment; and by increasing the likelihood of ongoing criminal justice involvement" (Harris, Evans, and Beckett 2010: 1756). Finally, keeping in touch with an incarcerated family member by making phone calls, visiting, and sending packages is quite costly (Comfort 2007: 284). It is difficult to estimate the cost of keeping in touch with a family member because most studies are based on families who are visiting a loved one (and, hence, we lack an estimate of how much it costs just to keep up with a family member via calls, packages, and letters), but the consensus is that the costs are steep (Comfort 2008; for estimates, see Braman 2004: 133; Grinstead et al. 2001: 64). Perhaps unsurprisingly, then, incarceration increases the difficulty that the remaining family members face covering bills such as rent and electricity (Schwartz-Soicher, Geller, and Garfinkel 2011), possibly even destabilizing their housing, as happened for many of the families in the qualitative data.

When asked how incarceration had affected their families, all families reported that it had worsened an already precarious financial situation, consistent with the existing research on the financial consequences of incarceration.

> Financially, most definitely. 'Cause I'm looking for a second job right now. Buying food, my rent going up, you know, just bills.
>
> — MICHELLE JOHNSON, *Biological mother of two*

> I think I killed three cars the whole time. We just had to sell a car for financial reasons.
>
> — NINA HOWARD, *Biological mother of two*

> It's [the financial stress] taken away our ability to deal with anything.... It's not like it's just that one thing... it's over and over and over.
>
> — ALLISON FREEMAN, *Biological mother of two*

Stories such as these describe incarceration as exacerbating parental stress associated significant financial struggles. And awareness of financial struggles was also a common point of discussion among children in the interviews (see also Nesmith and Ruhland 2008). Several children, some as young as nine (but many older), expressed a desire to contribute to the financial maintenance of the family, and all were acutely aware of the precariousness of their circumstances.

> We finally got our payments down for our mortgage and I was trying to get the budget figured out. How we can pay for everything each month.
>
> — KEVIN FREEMAN, *Age 17*

Colin Smith's grandmother, Barbara, also spoke about Colin's desire to help out the family financially at a relatively young age.

> He sees that, financially, we struggle. He's aware of it, he says he wants to get a job, get my license, get my permit; he wants to work.
>
> —BARBARA, *Regarding colin, age 12*

For most families in the qualitative data, the incarceration of a father continued or exacerbated a long-term trend of poverty and struggle. Of the families interviewed for a fourth time in 2006, all were receiving some form of public assistance, and five of eight were interviewed in public housing developments (suggesting that, as in the FFCW data, declines in father contributions are made up from other institutional sources (Sugie 2012)). Financial uncertainty may also cause or exacerbate stress and mental health problems. Allison Freeman, for example, described the bureaucratic hassles involved in keeping her home and obtaining public health and welfare assistance for herself and her children as "exhausting." Ms. Freeman also linked worry over losing her home to mental health problems in herself and her children throughout her interviews saying, "We are poverty stricken and that's been the hardest thing. I think there's been a lot of depression."

Ms. Freeman's children repeatedly described her as "stressed out," "aggravated," and "nervous," consistent with her depiction of herself as depressed. This picture, moreover, is consistent with findings of previous qualitative work. Ethnographic research in the United States paints a harrowing picture of the mental health and well-being of women left behind by incarcerated men (see also Wildeman, Schnittker, and Turney 2012). As Donald Braman (2004: 197), for instance, notes, "Nearly without exception, the women I spoke with who were closest to a prisoner had experienced depression and related their depression, at least in part, to the incarceration of their loved one." Similarly, Megan Comfort

(2008: 151) notes that one of the women in her study "became homeless due to incapacitating depression after her husband's trial and at the time of her interview had been living for nearly three months in a tent in a public campground with her children and grandchildren."

Comments like Ms. Freeman's and observations like those relayed by contemporary ethnographers (Braman 2004; Comfort 2008) and others (see e.g., Turnanovic, Rodriguez, and Pratt 2012; Wildeman, Schnittker, and Turney 2012; Sugie 2012; Hagan and Foster 2012; Siegel 2011) should not come as a surprise. As we demonstrated in chapter 2, the incarcerated (and their families) are disproportionately drawn from a pool of the most disadvantaged of citizens, and living in poverty is stressful. Extant research commonly describes consequences of incarceration that reverberate well beyond the inmate to their families. In the qualitative interviews, both caregivers and children blamed financial stress for increased conflict between caregiver and child, mental health problems in both groups, and a general sense of living in crisis. The FFCW data show similar consequences in parenting practices, relationship quality, and household instability. Taken together, these observations show that paternal incarceration not only can be harmful but may also have effects on such varied outcomes as physical and mental health and financial and housing stability.

It is also worth noting that the families of incarcerated men tend to withdraw from social networks in ways that make them less able to rely on informal supports should they need to call on kith or kin in a time of need. The qualitative interviews are replete with examples of this; children describe rejection by peers and difficulty reconciling an often positive father-child relationship with the stigma associated with the father's criminal involvement. In response to this contradiction, both children and caregivers described withdrawal from potential sources of social support as well as active efforts to hide the father's imprisonment. Indeed, as Donald Braman (2004: 171) notes, "Perhaps the most significant consequence of stigma among families of prisoners…is the distortion, diminution, and even severance of social ties." In considering the consequences of paternal incarceration for children, therefore, it is worth keeping in mind that the mechanisms that can drive any relationship need not be just hard shifts, but also softer ones, like stigma, which spill out in ways harmful to the social ties and emotional well-being of both mothers and children.

We began this chapter with a theoretical puzzle, noting that there are good reasons to suspect all sorts of paternal incarceration effects for children but that the direction of these relationships remained uncertain. We have shown that just because parents are disproportionately from disadvantaged minority groups, have low levels of educational attainment, and are unmarried, it does not mean that their absence will help their children. Indeed, as a substantial literature on child development suggests, the loss of a parent, and family instability more generally, is harmful to child well-being (Sik Kim 2011; Bowlby 1988; Rutter 1972; Fomby and Cherlin 2007). Many might still argue that parental incarceration is a special case of parental loss (and we agree). Yet, consider that children do not seem to benefit from the loss of a parent through entry into foster care—a transition that signals problem parenting as much or more than parental incarceration does. Like paternal incarceration, entry into foster care is not the boon to childhood well-being one might expect, even if children experienced significant neglect and trauma in their homes of origin (Doyle Jr. 2007, 2008). In some extreme cases, of course, the loss of a violent or abusive parent can help children, but this is not the norm for the average child. Based on the data we present here, we see good reason to think that the average child is harmed by paternal incarceration and that the effects may be large.

In the chapters that follow, we also attend to the empirical issues of selection and spuriousness. We have seen considerable evidence that children of incarcerated fathers would have fared worse than other children even if their father had never been incarcerated and that any relationship we may find between father incarceration and child outcomes is due to selection. Perhaps the most salient example of the problem is the case of Nathaniel Maxwell, the young man who introduced this chapter (and the book) by describing his parents, both of whom served several prison terms throughout his childhood, as "crackheads and alcoholics." Nathaniel was arguably doing the worst of all of the children we interviewed; yet it is clear that paternal incarceration is the least of his problems. In 2004, at age eleven, Nathaniel was attending a school for children with behavioral and emotional problems. He had been placed in the school after making a series of assaults on other students in his prior school and was under supervision of a parole officer by 2005. He reports that he joined a gang at age twelve and was arrested for armed robbery, assault, and drug selling. In 2006, at the age of fourteen, Nathaniel was interviewed while incarcerated in the most secure juvenile correctional facility in the state. For Nathaniel, the reasons his father and mother ended up in jail are the same reasons he finds himself incarcerated. He attributes no *direct* influence to his father's (or mother's) imprisonment on his life:

> INTERVIEWER: How do you think your life would be different [if your father had not gone to prison]?
>
> NATHANIEL: It'd probably still be the same. I'm assuming because both of them were crackheads and alcoholics. My biological mom, all of her sons and daughters were in foster homes or her family understood that she couldn't take care of 'em.

What is striking about Nathaniel is not paternal incarceration per se but how much of his own biography is shared with his father's. Both joined gangs, amassed criminal records that involved violent crimes, and were under correctional supervision by the age of twelve. Rather than a cause of Nathaniel's current problems, parental imprisonment in this case is more likely the result of the extreme disadvantages both father and son faced. Yet Nathaniel's case, like the descriptions of abuse evident in the FFCW data or in the Freeman and Harrison case studies, is not the norm. Most children of incarcerated parents do not themselves end up in prison, and most incarcerated parents do not have the problems Nathaniel's parents had. While it is important to account for cases like Nathaniel's, it does not then follow that his case is typical for the average child of the prison boom.

CONCLUSION

When we first developed an interest in parental incarceration, we saw at least three reasons that considering the effects of parental incarceration on children could be an important endeavor. First, previous research on mass incarceration suggested that having ever been incarcerated did significant harm not only to the earnings of adult men (for example, Western 2006; Pager 2003) but also to their families (Nurse 2002; Braman 2004). If incarceration affected both the earnings and family lives of incarcerated men, couldn't it also have consequences for their children? Second, at the time we began conceiving this project, the sheer volume of parents passing through prisons each year and the dramatic racial and class inequalities in the risk of parental imprisonment suggested that the prison boom could increase racial inequalities in childhood—provided parental incarceration harms children. Finally, we realized that the erratic nature of contemporary imprisonment, with its cycling of inmates from prison to community, took on added meaning when one considers that most inmates are parents (Petersilia 2003; Mumola 2000).

Despite these reasons to concentrate on parental incarceration, research on the topic is relatively new. Theory and public debate on the issue is by no means clear in its predictions. Many might, for example, begin with an assumption that children will be better off when their parents go to prison. Viewed from this perspective, prison may be a *cause of improvement* in the lives of children. On the other hand, bad parents may be *selected into prison*, suggesting that the absence of this parent will not influence the life chances of children for good or ill. In sorting out whether prison causes improvement for children or merely serves to select bad parents out of their homes, it is meaningful that both of these arguments rely on two related and erroneous assumptions. First, both arguments assume that parents who go to prison are bad parents. Given their criminal activity, the incarcerated, on average, are not exemplary parents. But it does not follow that inmates do nothing positive for their children. In the qualitative interviews described here, fathers were described as wholly problematic in only two of the eight families highlighted. The FFCW data similarly reveal heterogeneity in parenting within this population, although the quantitative data suggest that even somewhat fewer incarcerated parents may be primarily harmful to their children. Second, both the positive and selection arguments ignore the range of possible outcomes for children as a direct result of imprisonment. Even if an inmate is a lax or irresponsible parent, it would seem to matter if incarceration causes a child to enter foster care as opposed to a stable home with another family member. Similarly, even if parental drug selling is bad for children, the imprisonment of a parent may coincide with a considerable drop in the financial resources available to the child or an increase in conflict with the primary caregiver.

Why do we suspect that incarceration will, on average, harm children? First and foremost, we expect negative effects on children because inmates are parents like any others and there is significant heterogeneity in their experiences. Some are invested in their children and others are not. Some are successful in parenting and others struggle. While the nature of the average influence of inmate parents remains to be seen, we find it implausible that they have no effect based on the data described here. Immature and irresponsible parents may present difficulties for their children, but they may not be wholly bad parents. Foster care placement again represents a relevant example. Entry into the foster care system is harmful for children, even when they experienced significant trauma in their home of origin (Doyle Jr. 2007, 2008). Contrast this with parental imprisonment, where entry into prison is rarely the result of parents abusing or victimizing their child. Viewed from this perspective, parental imprisonment is not, a priori, synonymous with bad parenting, and there is reason to think that more children are harmed by the experience than helped by it.

It is especially important to recognize that even the worst examples of fatherhood in the qualitative data are not representative of the average incarcerated father. It would certainly make sense that the children of violent sex offenders experience paternal incarceration rather differently than the children of drug dealers, but violent sex offenders represent a small proportion of the pool of incarcerated fathers. Mr. Harrison and Mr. Freeman are simply not typical of the fathers incarcerated during the prison boom. While slightly more than half of all men incarcerated in state facilities were sent there for violent crimes in 2009, less than 15 percent were incarcerated for violent sex crimes (Sourcebook of Criminal Justice Statistics 2011). Incarcerated men in the contemporary era are much more likely to be inconsistent parents, often with drug problems, like Mr. Smith or Mr. Maxwell. There are also likely to be a fair number of Terence Howards in today's prisons; men for whom personal and structural constraints limit their ability to provide for their families through legal means but who nonetheless value their roles as fathers.

Second, as we noted at the outset, assumptions about inmate parents and their effects on children suffer from an unfair comparison. To take one example, research highlights maternal depression as a key factor determining childhood well-being (Turney 2011). The relevant comparison here is between kids with a depressed mother and those with a mother who is present but not depressed. The relevant comparison is *not* between children with a depressed mother and those with no mother at all. By arguing that maternal depression is problematic for kids, scholars do not suggest that children would be better off if their depressed mothers moved away and visited them sporadically. By the same logic, to argue that the criminal involvement of parents is problematic for children is not to say that children would be better off if the criminal parent disappeared. A positive parent-child relationship can buffer children from all sorts of problems, even those that involve parental substance use, mental illness, or significant poverty (all common to incarcerated parents).

Third, assumptions about inmate parents suffer from a troubling inattention to the challenges induced by incarceration. Children of incarcerated parents are at greater risk for poverty as well as for the myriad stresses and strains that come with living in poverty. Additionally, it is not poverty or parental unemployment per se that causes poor outcomes for children. Rather, it is neighborhood context, stress, conflict, and the declines in parenting quality that tend to accompany economic disadvantage that drive outcomes for children (Menaghan 1997; Duncan and Brooks-Gunn 1997; Brooks-Gunn, Duncan, and Aber 1997). That most children of incarcerated parents will be moved to stable, financially secure homes following a parent's imprisonment is unlikely at best.

Finally, it is worth recalling just who the inmates of the prison boom are and what caused them to be incarcerated in the first place. The prison boom resulted primarily (though not solely) from the increased use and lengthening of prison sentences for less serious offenders. The average incarcerated parent today is a less serious offender than in years past. If prisons selected only the most serious offenders, we would have completely different expectations about how incarceration would influence children. However, the current population of inmates—the downtrodden but less often dangerous—suggest the overlap between involved parent and incarcerated parent may be much larger in the mass incarceration era. This suggests that parental incarceration is a meaningful and potentially harmful event in the life course of the most disadvantaged children. Parental incarceration helps some children. It has no effect on others. But as the quantitative and qualitative data in this chapter show, it more often serves to make a bad situation worse.

PATERNAL INCARCERATION AND

MENTAL HEALTH AND

BEHAVIORAL PROBLEMS

IN THIS CHAPTER, we highlight the consequences of paternal incarceration for childhood well-being, broadly defined as children's internalizing, externalizing, physically aggressive, and total behavioral problems. We focus on these broad measures of mental health and behavioral problems for several reasons. Perhaps most important, while many observers point to the proportion of current inmates with parents who served time (Uggen and Wakefield 2005; Hagan and Palloni 1990), not all (or even most) children of inmates will ever be incarcerated. A solitary focus on criminal justice involvement is not only stigmatizing for the children of incarcerated parents; it also obscures significant unconsidered social harm—and relegates the experiences of female children to the background, since so few women experience incarceration.

We also focus on mental health and behavioral problems because they cover the full range of problems that most parents worry about. Every parent can relate to trying to make an aggressive child cooperative or an anxious child confident. And millions of parents can relate to the worries associated with how best to usher children through major life transitions, such as moving, financial difficulty, or divorce. Parents worry about mental health and behavioral problems in childhood for good reason. Especially at the extreme end of the continuum, and for the most disadvantaged children, mental health and behavioral problems are strong predictors of crime and delinquency later in the life course (Nagin and Tremblay 2001; Moffitt 1993). They also predict many other outcomes, including educational and occupational attainment and family formation (McLeod and Kaiser 2004; South 2002; Hagan and Wheaton 1993; Foster and Hagan 2007, 2009). In short, if paternal incarceration exacerbates children's behavioral and mental health problems today, we can expect it to exact measurable social costs tomorrow. By focusing on these types of problems, therefore, we provide indirect evidence concerning the long-term consequences of paternal incarceration for the children of the prison boom that we cannot provide directly because of the data limitations we discussed in the introduction.

Still, while mental health and behavioral problems are clearly important for later life outcomes, no childhood is perfect. And yet most children manage to grow up to be perfectly fine adolescents and adults. Indeed, criticism of today's "helicopter parents" often begins by noting that most parental worry is overblown. There is equally good evidence that children may benefit from (some) struggle because it fosters resilience and the development of coping strategies. Imagine, however, a child experiencing many stressors over a short period of time. How might a child who may tend toward aggression or anxiety anyway deal with a divorce, a move, and sudden financial instability all at once? How might an already vulnerable child cope with additional disadvantage? For these children, mental health and behavioral problems take on added meaning when we consider the power of childhood experiences to explain adult outcomes.

We showed in chapters 2 and 3 that the children of the prison boom are more likely to be disadvantaged before their parent was locked up. Now, we ask whether the additional problems imposed by parental incarceration result in greater mental health and behavioral problems for these children. Throughout, we shift our focus from parental incarceration generally to the consequences of paternal incarceration specifically. Doing this is appropriate for a number of reasons. First, the vast majority of children who experience parental incarceration experience the imprisonment of a father, not a mother (see figures 2.2 and 2.3 in chapter 2). Second, because maternal incarceration remains rare even among the poorest families, with many of the available data sets, it is difficult to generate sufficient statistical power to generate stable estimates of effects. More importantly for our purposes, the rare experience of maternal incarceration is therefore unlikely to be a cause of social inequality—even if it has large negative effects on children—because an event must be common and must do harm to be a driver of inequality (Wildeman and Muller 2012).

Finally, we focus on imprisonment of fathers because the evidence linking maternal incarceration to mental health and behavioral outcomes in children is thin. This may come as a surprise to many, given that incarcerated mothers are more likely to be living with their children prior to incarceration (Mumola 2000) and the generally large responsibility for childrearing we assign to mothers (relative to fathers) in our culture. We suspect the null effects of maternal incarceration on children's outcomes likely result from the large distributional differences in the profiles of incarcerated men and women, which is a fancy way of saying that women who end up behind bars are, on average, struggling with more serious problems than are men who end up behind bars, many of which further complicate the mother's parenting. As we noted in the introduction, the prison boom had the effect of drawing less serious offenders into the prison system, at least among men. The boom has affected women as well: rates of women's imprisonment increased even more rapidly than those for men in recent decades, but we are still talking about a small number of incarcerated women with very serious problems. In 2011, for example, men were imprisoned at roughly fourteen times the rate of women, corresponding to roughly 1.38 million more men behind bars relative to women (Carson and Sabol 2012). Looked at in this way, it should come as no surprise that the effects of maternal incarceration on children are dwarfed by existing disadvantages before imprisonment (see e.g., Siegel 2011), isolated to a small number of outcomes (see e.g., Cho 2009 a, b), and more often than not null (Wildeman and Turney forthcoming). None of this suggests that maternal incarceration is unimportant; only that it is unlikely to be relevant for large-scale shifts in racial inequality caused by the prison boom.[1]

CHOOSING THE DATA

Having explained our focus on mental health and behavioral problems among the children of incarcerated fathers, we now turn to a detailed discussion of our choice of data and analytic strategy in the interest of providing a sufficiently detailed discussion that will also explain the decisions we make in the later chapters that try to identify effects on infant mortality and child homelessness. Few national or representative surveys include detailed information on paternal incarceration. The data that do exist have a variety of strengths and weaknesses. We review these here to demonstrate why we have chosen the most appropriate data sets possible.

Although no large-scale data set includes extensive information on the children of incarcerated fathers and mothers, several longitudinal data sets ask a small set of questions about the incarceration of a father. The National Longitudinal Study of Adolescent Health (hereafter, Add Health), a nationally representative school sample of American seventh graders to twelfth graders in 1994–1995, asks whether and approximately when a father was incarcerated (Harris et al. 2009).[2] Similarly, the Cambridge Study in Delinquent Development ([CSDD]; Farrington 1994) follows eight- and nine-year-old boys who were registered in Cambridge schools in 1961 and includes extensive information on exposure to the criminal justice system. For the analyses presented here, however, we leave aside both Add Health and the CSDD in favor of the Project on Human Development in Chicago Neighborhoods (PHDCN) and the FFCW study (Earls et al. 2002; Reichman et al. 2001).

The FFCW and the PHDCN are longitudinal surveys of children and their primary caregivers: in the FFCW, of young children (ages five and under for the wave of data we analyze); and in the the PHDCN, of children and adolescents (ages six to fifteen for the waves of data we analyze). The PHDCN followed roughly six thousand children, adolescents, and young adults in Chicago over three waves of data collection from 1994 to 2002. The FFCW followed roughly five thousand children born between 1998 and 2000 in twenty large cities, and interviewed both parents when possible, a key benefit since it means we have multiple sources of information on the father's incarceration. The initial interviews for the FFCW were conducted with parents in hospitals shortly after the mother gave birth. Parents were interviewed again approximately twelve, twenty-four, and sixty months later. In addition to providing rich contextual information about the characteristics of the child's home, family, neighborhood, and school, both data sets also include information on the incarceration of family members. Each data source asks about current, recent, and prior paternal incarceration, allowing us to precisely estimate the effects of paternal incarceration on children.[3] Childhood mental health and behavioral problems are common to both the data sets we consider and allow causal estimates for a wide age range of vulnerable children and adolescents.

We focus on the PHDCN and the FFCW data because among the available data sets they strike the best balance between representing the experiences of the children of the prison boom and providing high-quality, repeated measures of childhood disadvantage, behavioral and mental health problems, and paternal incarceration. Although some other studies, such as the CSDD, include more nuanced measures of criminal justice contact (and a substantially longer follow-up period), and others, such as Add Health, are more broadly representative, the PHDCN and the FFCW offer representativeness (which allows our point estimates to apply to a broad range of the population), timeliness (which allows us to focus directly on the children of the prison boom), and a high quality of repeated measures (which makes us confident that our point estimates are as close to representing causal estimates as possible using observational data).[4,5] As we progress in the chapter, it should become transparent just how high the data demands are for estimating the effects of paternal incarceration on children; we stress these benefits now because merely showing associations between the incarceration of a father and children's behavioral and mental health problems tells us little about how mass imprisonment shapes future inequality.

Our choice to use the FFCW and PHDCN data sets comes at a cost, however, as neither data set is ideally suited to telling us how the incarceration of a father affects his children's later outcomes in the life course, such as their schooling or occupational attainment. The FFCW children are still quite young, and as such their schooling outcomes provide little more insight into their long-term well-being than do measures of their behavioral and mental health. Although they are older, the PHDCN children's schooling outcomes were measured in a way that it makes it very difficult to confidently isolate the effects of paternal incarceration. The same is the case for a host of other interesting outcomes, such as teenage pregnancy, delinquency and arrest, and dropping out of high school. Nevertheless, since we consider a broad range of measures of behavioral and mental health problems, our analyses in this chapter provide wide-ranging insight into how these children should fare in each of these important dimensions as their lives unfold.

DESCRIPTIVE DIFFERENCES BETWEEN CHILDREN OF INCARCERATED FATHERS AND OTHER CHILDREN

How different are the outcomes of children of incarcerated fathers from those of other children? Figure 4.1 shows striking differences in behavioral and mental health problems between children

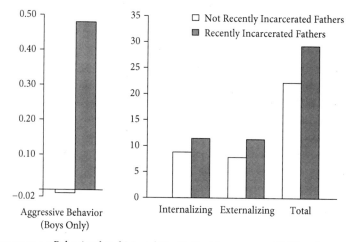

FIGURE 4.1 Behavioral and Mental Health Problems among Children by Recent Paternal Incarceration

Source: Fragile Families & Child Wellbeing Study (Aggressive Only); Project on Human Development in Chicago Neighborhoods (all others)

of recently incarcerated parents and other children, with children of incarcerated fathers faring worse, on average, on all four of the broad types of outcomes we consider here. Based on our analyses of the PHDCN data, the children of the incarcerated exhibit 30 percent more internalizing behavioral problems (11.45 to 8.81), 44 percent more externalizing behavioral problems (11.32 to 7.83), and 33 percent more total behavioral problems (29.49 to 22.23) than do other children. In our analyses of the FFCW data, boys with recently incarcerated fathers were also about one-half standard deviation more physically aggressive than other boys (.49 to −.01).[6]

Yet, the fact that children of recently incarcerated fathers exhibit far more behavioral and mental health problems than other children does not necessarily mean that the incarceration of the father causes those problems. This is easy to say but hard to illustrate, so we supplement the work we did in chapter 3 by providing a more extensive list of the ways these children and their family lives differed from each other before their father was incarcerated (or not) in figures 4.2 and 4.3. We focus on these specific background characteristics because we considered them sufficiently important to adjust for them in the statistical models reviewed later.

Perhaps the most notable difference is that in both of the data sets we use, children of recently incarcerated parents exhibited more behavioral and mental health problems than did other children even before their father was incarcerated, suggesting that selection into parental incarceration is likely driving some of these differences. The sole exception is for internalizing behaviors in the PHDCN data, where the differences are small and in the opposite direction than we would have expected (though the difference is not statistically significant and therefore should be thought of as no discernible difference). Still, the differences between children of recently incarcerated fathers and other children grow—sometimes substantially—between the two interviews, suggesting that

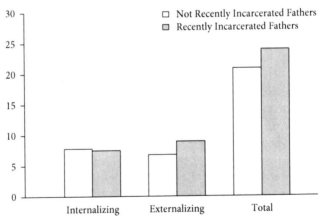

FIGURE 4.2 Previous Behavioral Problems by Recent Paternal Incarceration
Source: Project on Human Development in Chicago Neighborhoods

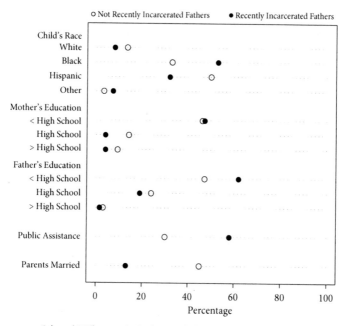

FIGURE 4.3 Selected Differences in Background Characteristics among Children by Recent Paternal Incarceration in the PHDCN

Source: Project on Human Development in Chicago Neighborhoods

the incarceration of the father may drive some of the differences. Nonetheless, the differences in the baseline behaviors of the groups suggest that establishing that some of these differences are due to paternal incarceration will be difficult.

The baseline differences between children who later have a father incarcerated and those who do not reflect preexisting disadvantages and are consequential for mental health and behavioral problems. Figure 4.3 displays a selection of these among children in the PHDCN. As we showed in chapter 2, children who later have a father incarcerated are far more likely to be African American and to have low-education fathers (and, albeit to a lesser degree, mothers). They are also much more

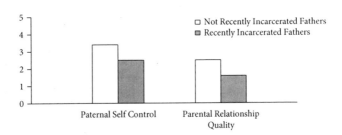

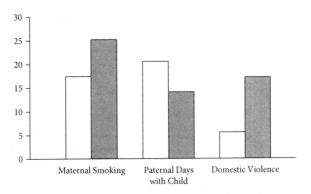

FIGURE 4.4 Background Characteristics by Recent Paternal Incarceration
Source: Fragile Families & Child Wellbeing Study

likely to receive public assistance and to have unmarried parents, both important correlates of mental health and behavioral problems.

Similar problems, again highly correlated with mental health and behavioral problems, are present among children in the FFCW, as shown in figure 4.4. Even prior to incarceration, their fathers scored, on average, lower on measures of self-control, parental relationship quality, and days spent with their children. Children with a father who will later be incarcerated are also more likely to have mothers who smoke and to be exposed to domestic violence.

Figures 4.2, 4.3, and 4.4 present good reasons to think that many problems of children of incarcerated parents would persist, even if their fathers had never gone to prison or jail. Yet, despite the other obstacles these children face, paternal incarceration may still do them harm. Maybe most telling in this regard is that the descriptive comparisons show larger differences between the children of incarcerated fathers after incarceration than prior to incarceration. These descriptive differences suggest that an analysis of the effect of paternal incarceration is warranted but that it will be important to address issues of selection and preexisting disadvantages.

ESTIMATING THE EFFECT OF PATERNAL INCARCERATION ON CHILDREN

Although it is relatively easy, given a good data source, to compare children of incarcerated parents to their peers, these naïve comparisons tell us nothing about what role, if any, incarceration played in determining the observed differences. Are they attributable to a true causal effect of paternal incarceration? Or are they simply a reflection of the various family and individual traits that led to the parent's incarceration in the first place? Could paternal incarceration be protective? In short, would the child's behavioral and mental health problems have been better, worse, or no different had the father never experienced incarceration? Based on research on the effects of incarceration on men and on the harmful effects of incarceration on family life we showed in chapter 3, we expect incarceration to have played a key role— even above and beyond the damaging consequences of having a parent arrested or convicted of a crime. Yet, based on the other differences between children soon to experience a father's incarceration and not soon to do so, it is also reasonable to expect null or even positive effects in some instances, especially when there is evidence that the father had been physically abusive to family members.

The main challenges for our analysis are that fathers are not randomly assigned to prison, and the factors that predict paternal incarceration also predict poor child outcomes. We therefore use several methods to estimate the effect of imprisonment. Similarity in the direction and magnitude of the effects of paternal incarceration across various modeling strategies, data sets, and measures represents one important robustness test of the arguments we make here. Interested readers may investigate the methodological appendix at the back of the book for the details of our modeling strategies. We begin here with a brief discussion of the difficulties involved in the analysis and describe intuitively what we did to produce high-quality—and likely quite conservative—estimates of the effects of paternal imprisonment on children.

Many Methods for Isolating Incarceration Effects

In this section, we consider methods that can be used to try to tease out evidence that incarceration *causes* changes in the lives of children. Rather than comparing across children at one point in time, the question necessitates *within-individual* comparisons, focusing on whether or not parental incarceration imposes an additional strain on already-stressed children.

As chapter 3 suggests, there are many ways that incarceration may affect children, some negative and some positive. The trauma of witnessing an arrest, the absence of an involved parent, or the stress on the primary caregiver left behind is likely to affect a child (Comfort 2007). By the same token, the removal of a parent who has severe substance abuse problems, mental health problems, or other problems common to the incarcerated population, such as abuse, may make children better off—or at least have no discernible effects on them. We focus our attention on the average effect of incarceration on children and offer an analysis of the *net effect* of paternal incarceration. Using the FFCW data, we also test whether domestic violence moderates the effects of paternal incarceration on children's physically aggressive behaviors.

It would be much easier to identify the effects of parental incarceration on children if we could randomly assign parents to prison. This, of course, is impossible and unethical, so social scientists are left with a number of imperfect strategies. Absent random assignment, analysts can try to measure all possible co-occurring causes of mental health and behavioral problems (e.g., poverty) that are also related to imprisonment and control for them in a statistical model, thus netting out other factors and isolating the effect of parental imprisonment. This strategy has several problems. In practice, surveys never include every possible measure of interest, and a creative analyst can always hypothesize an omitted variable that might dramatically bias the results. Of larger concern is that social scientists, especially in an emerging area where little is known about the topic, often simply don't know what they don't know. The strategy of measuring and controlling for other variables is unattractive because we will never know with certainty when we have succeeded in "controlling for" everything that matters.

Having discarded experimental manipulation as unethical and covariate adjustment as less than ideal, we are left with four strategies for estimating the effects of parental incarceration on children. The first, called *propensity score matching*, is designed to ensure an appropriate comparison among children by using a two-stage process to eliminate comparisons between children whose fathers had no chance of incarceration with those whose fathers had a high chance of incarceration (Rosenbaum and Rubin 1983; Winship and Morgan 1999).[7] Assuming that there are no unobserved differences between children who do and do not have a father incarcerated, propensity score models improve on covariate adjustment by allowing a researcher to match persons on a variety of characteristics (such as race, age, gender, and employment status), thereby making an "apples to apples" comparison rather than just adjusting for a host of different covariates. Put most simply, propensity score models compare the mental health of children with fathers who had a high (or low) likelihood of entering prison *and did* with children whose fathers had a high (or low) likelihood of entering prison *and did not.*

The second strategy used to estimate the direct effects of paternal incarceration on children are *fixed-effect,* or *within-person, change models.* These models improve upon the comparison problem in the prior models by estimating the effect of incarceration on *changes* in mental health or behavioral problems in children. In other words, instead of trying to ensure appropriate comparisons *across children,* fixed-effect models make within-child comparisons, comparing a child's mental health before a father is incarcerated with his or her mental health afterward. The largest challenge with these models is that they require longitudinal data and repeated measures of relevant variables—a requirement that is not often met in conjunction with large-scale survey data. The most vital contribution of this specific model is that no variables related to selection into treatment and mental health that remain stable can bias the results.

A third strategy, called a *placebo (or synthetic) regression,* seeks to increase our confidence in the results by showing that we do not see effects where we could not or should not see them. This method can be applied by using implausible timing, such as using *future* incarceration to *predict* current child behavior, or implausible outcomes, such as predicting changes in height as a result of paternal incarceration, to show that we do not see effects where we could not or should not see them. Although this method is not commonly used, we see it as a natural addition to the modeling strategies utilized throughout the other analyses in this chapter.

Finally, where possible, we reproduce our paternal incarceration models on a limited sample of men who have been incarcerated before. We do this to demonstrate that the effects presented here are the result of incarceration, not of other events associated with arrest or differences in criminal propensities among incarcerated and nonincarcerated men. Skeptics, for example, might argue that arrest experiences or the initial receipt of a felony conviction drives the effects presented here, rather than the incarceration experience per se. They might also worry that the results are driven by preexisting criminal propensities, reflected in histories of criminal involvement, rather than incarceration. By limiting the sample to those who have been incarcerated before (and hence likely have a felony conviction and, presumably, higher than average criminal propensities), we show that paternal incarceration is consequential even for the children of fathers who are deeply involved in the criminal justice system.

Of course, none of the analytic strategies described here are perfect, nor do they completely eliminate the problems associated with selection bias. Propensity score models ensure appropriate comparisons, but they also suffer from omitted variable problems. Put simply, propensity score models can produce high-quality estimates only if fathers who do and do not go to prison do not differ in any ways beyond those that we observe. Fixed-effect models perform better with respect to comparisons but do not handle dynamic shifts associated with paternal incarceration well. So, these models perform well unless something else (such as employment status or drug use) changed in the lead-up to the father's incarceration that may have caused it.

We take the view that it is useful to analyze parental incarceration across a variety of analytic strategies and data sets. The effects of parental incarceration, fortunately, turn out to be remarkably similar regardless of strategy. We begin with a simple bivariate model estimating the baseline effect of paternal incarceration on mental health and behavioral outcomes ("descriptive models"). We then include controls for factors influencing selection into prison (e.g., those displayed in figures 4.3 and 4.4). As mentioned earlier, we do not expect these models to estimate causal effects. Rather, they serve as a descriptive indication of how the behavioral and mental health problems of children of incarcerated parents compare to those of other children. We then proceed to more rigorous estimation procedures, including lagged dependent variable, fixed-effect, and propensity score models (see the methodological appendix for more detail).

Each of these strategies represents a substantial—although imperfect—advance over simple regression models in the estimation of causal effects using observational data. That said, we take care to be appropriately cautious throughout our discussion and only call attention to those results that stand up to rigorous analysis and hold across all strategies, data sets, and models. We also reproduce the effects from the FFCW data with a limited sample of ever-incarcerated fathers (figure 4.7). We then test for implausible effects with placebo regressions using the FFCW data (figure 4.8). We close by considering whether domestic violence or offense type moderates these effects in the FFCW data, to see if some children are harmed more by paternal incarceration, some less (figure 4.9). Throughout the discussion of the results, we have avoided any additional discussion of the statistical nitty gritty of these models, but, again, interested readers may consult the methodological appendix for more detail on these models.

DOES PATERNAL INCARCERATION HELP OR HURT CHILDREN?

In both data sets, children of incarcerated fathers were, even prior to the incarceration, worse off than their peers who had no father incarcerated. That the incarcerated are drawn primarily from disadvantaged segments of the population and that children of the incarcerated experience a host of deficits are well known. Thus, the bar is high for assessing whether paternal incarceration caused any of the gaps between children of incarcerated fathers and other children.

Figure 4.5 shows the results of all of these strategies using the PHDCN data; figure 4.6 does the same thing for the FFCW data. The figures present all the regression modeling strategies described earlier, progressing from (1) a baseline descriptive model to (2) one that includes controls for preexisting disadvantages and

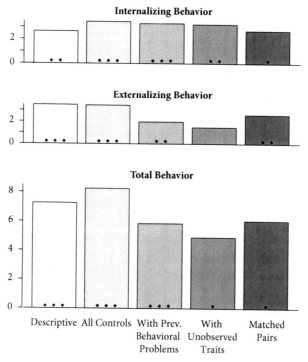

FIGURE 4.5 Comparison of Paternal Incarceration Effects Across Model Types

Notes: ***p < .001, **p < .01, *p < .05

Source: Project on Human Development in Chicago Neighborhoods

demographic characteristics ("all controls") to (3) lagged dependent variables models ("with previous behavior problems"), (4) fixed-effects models ("with unobserved traits"), and (5) propensity score models ("matched pairs").

The figures present a range of modeling strategies, outcomes, and measures and yet show remarkably similar results. In PHDCN analyses (figure 4.5), well-being indicators are measured with the Child Behavior Checklist ([CBCL]; Achenbach 1991). The CBCL can be scaled in a variety of ways; we focus here on the summary

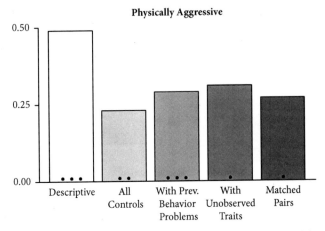

FIGURE 4.6 Comparison of Paternal Incarceration Effects across Model Types

Notes: ***p < .001, **p < .01, *p < .05

Source: Fragile Families & Child Wellbeing Study

scales measuring internalizing problems (such as depression or somatic complaints), externalizing problems (such as aggression or delinquency), and total behavioral problems, which encompasses both types. In the FFCW analyses (figure 4.6), the measure is a narrower gauge of children's physical aggression, which includes how often the child destroys things that belong to other people, gets into fights, and attacks people. Although narrow, this measure corresponds closely with measures intimately tied with criminality in adolescence and adulthood (Nagin and Tremblay 2001). The FFCW result refers to young boys, whereas the PHDCN results refer to older children and adolescents of both sexes.[8]

In the PHDCN, the basic descriptive model suggests that children with recently incarcerated fathers exhibit 2.64 more internalizing behaviors than children who did not have a father incarcerated recently, a statistically significant difference. Of course, this serves merely as a description of the differences between these two types of children, and, as we discussed earlier, these differences may be caused by something other than paternal incarceration. To address this possibility, we consider how adjusting for various covariates ("all controls") and an earlier measure of behavioral and mental health problems ("with previous behavioral problems") alters the relationship. In both cases, adjusting for these additional measures actually *increases* the size of the relationship between paternal incarceration and internalizing problems. Thus, models 2 ("all controls") and 3 ("with previous behavior problems") in figure 4.5 suggest that if anything, the effects of paternal incarceration on children's internalizing behaviors may be bigger than we suspected. While the relationship does fall to the level shown in the baseline model in the more rigorous propensity score ("matched pairs") model, the relationship still continues to be at least as large as the basic descriptive association and statistically significant in each case. Taken together, the results show that paternal incarceration increases children's internalizing behaviors.

Paternal incarceration could increase children's internalizing behavioral problems but have no effect on their externalizing behaviors. In the second row of figure 4.5, we test this relationship using the same five models. The basic bivariate model ("descriptive") and the model that just adjusts for observed covariates but not prior externalizing behaviors ("all controls") again reveal negative effects. In each case, recent paternal incarceration is associated with higher levels of externalizing behaviors among children. In other models, however, the findings for externalizing behaviors depart somewhat from the findings for internalizing behaviors. In model 3, which adjusts for prior externalizing behaviors, the relationship is cut 45 percent from what is shown in the baseline model, suggesting that some of the differences in externalizing behaviors between children of recently incarcerated fathers and other children were present before the father was incarcerated, as our findings in figure 4.2 suggested. In model 4, which adjusts for unobserved traits in children and families, the relationship between paternal incarceration and children's externalizing behaviors is reduced further—down 58 percent from the baseline model. Results from model 5, which utilizes matched pairs, demonstrate a stronger relationship than those found in model 3 ("prior behavioral problems") and 4 ("with unobserved traits"). In the matched pairs model, 75 percent of the original relationship identified between paternal incarceration and children's externalizing behaviors remains. Based on these five models, we conclude that somewhere in the region of half of the relationship between recent paternal incarceration and children's externalizing behaviors is likely due to incarceration.

Results for total behavioral problems echo those for internalizing and externalizing behaviors. In all five models, the relationship between recent paternal incarceration and children's total behavioral problems is statistically significant and substantial. And in no case do observed or unobserved factors explain more than about one-third of the relationship between recent paternal incarceration and children's total behavioral problems. Taken together, the results from figure 4.5 suggest a statistically significant and substantial negative relationship between recent paternal incarceration and children's behavioral problems. They suggest, furthermore, that no more than about half of this relationship is explained by factors other than recent paternal incarceration, suggesting that paternal incarceration does children substantial harm.

Results from the FFCW, which consider the relationship between paternal incarceration and young boys' physical aggression using the same modeling strategies utilized for the PHDCN, point to similar harm associated with recent paternal incarceration. In the baseline model in figure 4.5, which shows the descriptive relationship between paternal incarceration and boys' physically aggressive behaviors, suggests that boys of recently incarcerated fathers engage in about .49 more physically aggressive behaviors than other boys, a difference that is highly significant. Adjusting for observable differences between families ("all controls"), including prior physical aggression ("with previous behavior problems"), cuts the relationship in half. But the relationship continues to be highly significant, pointing toward the damaging effects of a father's incarceration. Even in the most rigorous models ("with unobserved traits" and "matched pairs"), the relationship between paternal incarceration and boys' physically aggressive behaviors is never cut by more than 50 percent. The results from the FFCW parallel those from the PHDCN, as about half of the descriptive relationship between recent paternal incarceration and boys' physical aggression is explained by the experience of paternal incarceration.

The models described earlier represent the strongest possible modeling strategies, absent random assignment of parents to prison, to remove the sample selection bias problem from our estimates. They provide overwhelming evidence that paternal incarceration increases children's mental health and behavioral problems, even among children who were already at risk of difficulty. Other strategies for ruling out selection bias, including sample limitations and placebo regressions, yield the same results. The sample limitation strategy is shown in figure 4.7 and reproduces the models in figure 4.6 on a limited sample of fathers who

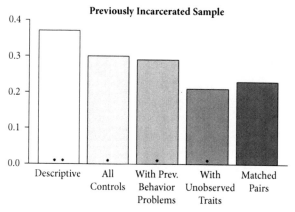

FIGURE 4.7 Comparison of Paternal Incarceration Effects across Model Types

Notes: ***p < .001, **p < .01, *p < .05

Source: Fragile Families & Child Wellbeing Study

had been incarcerated previously. By limiting the analysis to men who have already been incarcerated, we refute the argument that the results derive from other experiences related to contact with the criminal justice system (e.g., the trauma and stigma associated with arrest or felony conviction). It also refutes the argument that our results are the result of differences in criminal propensities among men who do and do not end up in prison—a sample of previously incarcerated men is likely to include *only those* with high levels of criminal propensity. Even among these men, an additional incarceration experience increases physically aggressive behaviors in their sons.

Another way to test the robustness of our results is to look for effects where there should not or could not be effects. In this instance, *not* finding implausible effects strengthens the case for the effects found earlier. We briefly summarize results from these "placebo regressions" utilizing paternal incarceration between a boy's third and fifth birthdays to predict his physical aggression at age three. Since the future cannot predict the past, finding any effects would suggest that our hypothesis is less plausible. In figure 4.8, we show the placebo results from variants of models 2 ("all controls")

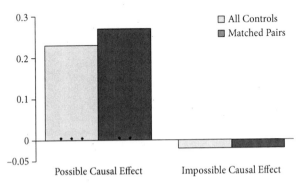

FIGURE 4.8 Results from True and Placebo Regression Models
Notes: ***p < .001, **p < .01, *p < .05
Source: Fragile Families & Child Wellbeing Study

and 5 ("matched pairs") from figure 4.6; we also include the true effect next to the placebo effect so that it is clear just how different these results are. The true model predicts a substantial increase in children's physical aggression as a result of their father's incarceration. The results from the placebo regression suggest that future paternal incarceration is associated with a tiny (7 percent of the true model), insignificant *decrease* in children's past aggression. In this model, we went looking for null effects and found null effects. In the true matched pairs model, we see significant, substantial effects on physically aggressive behaviors.

As the results to this point have demonstrated, across all age groups, paternal incarceration increases mental health and behavioral problems in children. The effects of paternal incarceration are global, increasing both externalizing problems (such as aggression and delinquency) and internalizing problems (such as anxiety and depression). Paternal incarceration results in approximately a one-third to one-half standard deviation increase in difficulties in all problems considered. It is also worth noting that nearly all the differences shown here were significant at the .05 level, with the lone exceptions of externalizing behaviors in the "unobserved traits" model of figure 4.4 and physically aggressive behaviors in the "unobserved traits" model in figure 4.7. Seeing effects where we expect to see them is encouraging. But it is also encouraging that we did not see effects where we did not expect to see them and that these effects largely hold even among a sample of previously incarcerated fathers.

Yet, consistent as the average effects are across a range of outcomes, from internalizing to externalizing to physically aggressive behaviors, some important variations bear mentioning. In the FFCW data, about 18 percent of recently incarcerated fathers were reported by the mother of their child to have engaged in domestic violence; for other men, rates of domestic violence were just over one-third that high (figure 4.4). Given the harmful effects of exposure to abuse on mother and child alike, it is worth considering whether paternal incarceration is moderated by domestic violence.

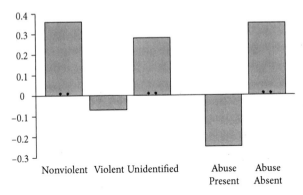

FIGURE 4.9 Effects of Recent Paternal Incarceration by Offense Type and in the Presence and Absence of Abuse

Notes: **p < .01

Source: Fragile Families & Child Wellbeing Study

Figure 4.9 presents versions of the lagged dependent variable models ("with previous behavior problems") from figure 4.6 that include interaction terms for domestic violence history and crime type.[9] The logic of an interaction term is straightforward. We essentially use this method to see whether the incarceration of a father has a significantly different effect when the father was abusive and when he was not. The findings from the model including this interaction term are striking. For fathers who were not reported to be abusive prior to their incarceration, the experience of incarceration is associated with a substantial and statistically significant increase in the physical aggression of their male children over what would have been expected if he had not gotten locked up. For these children, the incarceration of a father does real and significant harm. For children of fathers who were reported to have been abusive, however, this event is associated with a substantial *decrease* in their aggression, suggesting that the removal of a violent man from the household may enhance their well-being, or, since this effect is not statistically significant, does them no discernible harm. Results from the left panel of figure 4.9 paint a similar picture: all the effects we see here are concentrated among fathers incarcerated for nonviolent (and unidentified) offenses; for children whose fathers were convicted of violent offenses, their father's incarceration is associated with no discernible change in the physical aggression of these boys.

CONCLUSION

In this chapter, we have described the difficulties of studying the effects of parental incarceration on children and provided estimates of these effects. Detailing the mechanisms through which having a parent incarcerated causes mental health problems remains a considerable challenge. The effects of parental incarceration on children vary considerably, and researchers are just beginning to assess how and for whom parental incarceration is most consequential. One important consideration is relationship quality between the parents prior to incarceration. It is notable, for example, that the negative effect of paternal incarceration is observed *only* for children of fathers with no domestic-abuse history. A pure selection interpretation of our findings (and the findings of others) would predict just the opposite. If all observed effects of paternal incarceration were solely the result of selection bias, then we might expect the children of violent fathers to exhibit the highest level of behavioral problems. Instead, we observe little harm for these children after the incarceration of their fathers. Moreover, just as most inmates are not abusive and neglectful, neither is the average incarcerated father. In the FFCW, for example, rates of domestic abuse are generally higher than in the general population but not radically so.

The results presented in this chapter, strong and broad as they are, still provide little insight into how paternal incarceration shapes other risks in the lives of young children, such as their housing situations and their physical health, both of which are also of the utmost import for child well-being. Given how far-reaching the effects of behavioral and mental health problems are, we can imagine the effects of paternal incarceration on children to extend to these domains as well. Yet, without considering other outcomes, we cannot be sure whether paternal incarceration's consequences are limited to behavioral and mental health problems, or not. Likewise, the results from this chapter provide no insight into the consequences of mass imprisonment for future inequality. This experience compromises these children's life chances, to be sure, but it remains unclear how it affects subsequent inequality. We take up these considerations next.

PATERNAL INCARCERATION AND

INFANT MORTALITY

MOST PARENTS CAN recall a period when their child lacked self-control, seemed sad or anxious, or complained of a stomachache following a stressful event. Likewise, most parents can remember a time when a friend, family member, or teacher commented on how smart their child was—only to later wonder why he or she was having trouble learning the alphabet, the multiplication tables, or how to spell. That parental incarceration can exacerbate the sorts of problems common to childhood is important because so many of us relate to them. And yet, though the mental health and behavioral problems of children with an incarcerated parent may be similar to those of other children, they occur at much higher rates and tend to approach clinical levels. Take externalizing behaviors, for example. Most children act out from time to time in response to specific stressors, such as conflict within the family or the birth of a sibling; some are more prone to this sort of behavior than others. Children of the prison boom, however, are far more likely to exhibit levels of externalizing behaviors that suggest a need for clinical intervention. The difference between children of incarcerated parents and other children with respect to behavioral problems is therefore a matter of degree, not scope.

The elevated disadvantages prison boom children face also suggest that they might be at risk not only for the mental health or behavioral problems that many children face but also a host of other risks that, like parental incarceration, may be foreign to more advantaged children. In this chapter and the next, we consider two such outcomes: infant mortality and child homelessness. In so doing, we move from the common problems of childhood that children of incarcerated parents experience at more serious levels to rare events that few children ever experience but that have important implications for inequality and life chances. We focus on these events because they are tragic, all too common in the United States relative to other developed democracies, unequally distributed by race, and detrimental to children's long-term prospects.

Infant mortality—the death of a child before his or her first birthday—is the most consequential of all of the outcomes we consider. Whatever the problems and challenges of childhood, the death of a child so young is heartbreaking and renders all other problems moot. Every year, about 25,000 infants die in the United States. These deaths represent not just unrealized potential but also the pain of huge numbers of parents. While some of the causes of infant mortality are clear—birth defects or very low birth weight, for example—the facts remain: the United States has alarmingly high levels of infant mortality relative to other developed democracies, and race gaps in infant mortality rates stubbornly defy comprehensive explanation. Furthermore, the US infant mortality rate is even higher when we consider differences across countries in the proportion of children born healthy—that is, without birth defects tightly linked to infant mortality or so low birth weight that they are unlikely to survive—suggesting that other events in the first year of life might also explain some of the US infant mortality rate.

Infant mortality—or childhood homelessness, for that matter—differs from anxiety and aggression in another important, but perhaps less obvious, respect. We often tend to (incorrectly) write off anxiety or aggression in children as an essential trait, unresponsive to intervention. This is harder to do with infant mortality. Like most countries, the United States experienced a sharp decline in its infant mortality rate over the second half of the twentieth century (Singh 2007). Yet it still lags far behind the others in reducing infant mortality rates. That the United States has a high infant mortality rate despite the substantial gains made in other countries suggests that a number of policy interventions could reduce these rates. Similarly, that large race gaps remain an essential feature of infant mortality in this country is highly problematic and efforts to reduce them are difficult to disregard as unimportant.

PARENTAL INCARCERATION AND INFANT MORTALITY

Why focus on infant mortality in a book on the consequences of mass imprisonment for childhood inequality? Part of the answer is that our high infant mortality rate mirrors American exceptionalism with respect to imprisonment in several key respects. First, it exceeds that of all other similar long-standing democracies by at least 30 percent; absolute and relative declines in the American infant mortality rate have been smaller than those of similar nations over the last fifteen years (OECD 2006), as shown in figure 5.1. To highlight this slow rate of decline, consider that the American infant mortality rate slightly increased in 2002 when the rates of similarly situated nations continued a long-standing pattern of decline (MacDorman et al. 2005). Second, as with imprisonment, the black-white gap in the infant mortality rate remains substantial (Schempf et al. 2007; Wise 2003). In 2006, for example, the black infant mortality rate was 13.3 per 1,000; for whites, it was 5.6 per 1,000 (Heron et al. 2009). The black infant mortality rate in the United States is roughly in line with the infant mortality rates of Belarus, Sri Lanka, and Uruguay, countries that are not comparable to the United States on many other metrics. Third, as with imprisonment, there are vast state-level disparities and black-white disparities in the infant mortality rate (figure 5.1 and 5.2). These gaps have recently declined only a little, despite numerous interventions in urban America to try to combat some of the possible causes. The contours of American infant mortality thus suggest that the sources of this exceptionalism merit further investigation. We now consider mass incarceration as a novel explanatory factor.

Despite great interest in the consequences of parental incarceration for children and the causes of the high American infant

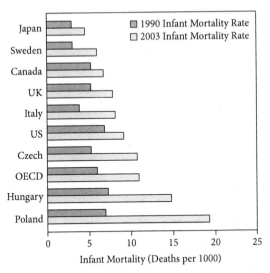

FIGURE 5.1 The Puzzle of American Infant Mortality
Source: Authors' calculation

mortality rate, no research has linked parental incarceration and infant mortality. Indeed, the very small body of research that attempts to link parental incarceration to offspring health outcomes focuses on effects seen in late adolescence and early adulthood (Roettger and Boardman 2012). Despite this, there are myriad reasons why a parent's incarceration could increase their infant's mortality risk.

One dominant perspective in public health, the *fundamental causes perspective*, links resources, broadly defined, to morbidity and mortality (Link and Phelan 1995, 2002). According to the fundamental causes perspective, the key mechanisms through which resources influence infant health and mortality are maternal health (Wise 2003) and access to technologies and information (Frisbie et al. 2004). Put simply, any event that substantially influences socioeconomic status is also likely to influence mortality; parental incarceration certainly fits the bill in each regard. While only a few

(a)

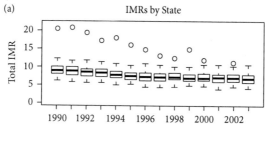

IMRs by State

(b)

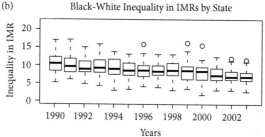

Black-White Inequality in IMRs by State

Years

FIGURE 5.2 Infant Mortality Rates and Black-White Inequality in Infant
Mortality, 1990–2003

Source: Authors' calculation

studies consider the effects of paternal incarceration on maternal
mental or physical health (Lee and Wildeman, Lee and Wildeman
2013; Lee et al., forthcoming; Wildeman, Schnittker, and Turney
2012), or of maternal incarceration on access to technologies,
health-promoting information, and better nutrition (Clarke and
Adashi 2011), the link between lack of resources and infant mortality is well-established. To influence the risk of infant mortality, parental incarceration must therefore diminish the resources
women have access to and/or affect their circumstances in ways
that directly imperil their mental and physical health.

As we have already noted, the diminished earnings associated with current and prior incarceration (Western 2006, 2002;
Pager 2003) and the elevated risk of union dissolution associated with a partner's incarceration (Lopoo and Western 2005;

Massoglia, Remster, and King 2011; Apel et al. 2010) combine to dramatically diminish paternal contributions to family life (Geller, Garfinkel, and Western 2011). Paternal incarceration also dramatically increases the costs families bear because the costs associated with maintaining contact with an incarcerated partner (Grinstead et al. 2001) and the additional child care and associated costs (Braman 2004) are often substantial (Comfort 2007). Since the socioeconomic pain of incarceration is transmitted to the partners, and since diminished resources are associated with elevated infant mortality risk, parental incarceration may increase this risk.

Beyond indirect influences on the resources women have available to them, having a partner incarcerated also directly influences maternal mental and physical health, both of which likely shape infant mortality. Most obviously, given the effects of prior incarceration on the risk of contracting an infectious disease (Massoglia 2008), having a partner incarcerated could increase women's risk of contracting such diseases. Indeed, macro-level research suggests that increases in the male incarceration rate have led to substantial increases in the female AIDS prevalence rate among African Americans (Johnson and Raphael 2009), plausibly due to the effects of incarceration on the probability of being in multiple sexual relationships concurrently (Khan et al. 2009). Incarceration may also compromise women's health by exposing them to higher levels of stress, which are well-known to increase the risk of cardiovascular disease (Lee et al., forthcoming). When the costs of having a partner incarcerated are combined with the damaging changes in his behavior upon his return (Goffman 2009; Nurse 2002) and the corrosive effects of incarceration on women's support networks (Braman 2004; Turney, Schnittker, and Wildeman 2012), the incarceration of a partner may inhibit maternal health (Lee and Wildeman, forthcoming).

Yet, despite these reasons to expect that paternal incarceration will increase the risk of infant mortality, some children may benefit from paternal incarceration—or at least suffer fewer of its consequences. As we showed in chapter 4, paternal incarceration seems to harm children only if the father had not been abusive toward the mother of his children. If the father was violent toward mother or children, then his absence does not appear to hurt—and may even help—children. On the face of it, this makes sense. As is the case for women exposed to a violent or otherwise abusive partner, it may be a relief to a child when the father is incarcerated (Comfort 2008; Nurse 2002), and the lower levels of stress that result from the incarceration of a violent partner might offset the decline in resources that result from incarceration, even leading to lower infant mortality risks.

TESTING THE PARENTAL INCARCERATION-INFANT MORTALITY RELATIONSHIP

Despite a strong theoretical basis linking parental imprisonment and infant mortality, no research has yet considered this relationship. Unfortunately, individual-level survey data containing a sufficient number of cases of parental incarceration and infant mortality to conduct statistical analyses are rare, meaning that the data limitations we face in this chapter are far, far greater than those we faced in the previous chapter. Traditional survey data are not suitable for considering the effects of imprisonment on infant mortality. Thankfully, one data set is: the Pregnancy Risk Assessment Monitoring System (PRAMS) data, which is run by the Center for Disease Control (CDC). Each year since 1988, participating states have contacted 1,300 to 3,400 women who gave birth in the last two to four months.[1] Although the PRAMS data, like the survey data described in chapter 4, are unique, they have limitations. First, surveys are completed an average of four months after the birth, so they do not provide a full measure of infant mortality. Second, they do not contain a measure of parental criminality, making it difficult to differentiate between effects of criminality and incarceration. There are also limited measures of family income and wealth, making it difficult to know whether poverty may be responsible for any association between parental incarceration and infant mortality. To deal with this concern, we limit our analysis to mothers who dropped out of high school. Since incarceration is concentrated among individuals with lower levels of education, this limits the sample to a group that is likely to experience the "treatment" of parental incarceration. In considering the parental incarceration–early infant mortality relationship, we use a measure of early infant mortality as the dependent variable that is based on maternal reports of whether the infant died before the interview. Although this is not a complete measure of infant mortality,[2] it is better than any measure of infant death in a large, representative data set that also measures parental incarceration.

Of course, it may be that any relationship between parental incarceration and early infant mortality is attributable to other measures of familial disadvantage, and not a real effect of parental incarceration. We adjust for all relevant background characteristics discussed in the research on the causes of infant mortality, including characteristics of the pregnancy and birth and the time since the birth (see the methodological appendix for more detail). As we mentioned in chapter 4, however, we are unable (because of data limitations) to run the full battery of statistical tests we used in considering effects on behavioral and mental health problems. Thus, although the analyses presented here are the strongest analyses of this relationship to date, our statements about causality in this chapter must be tempered relative to those in chapter 4, where we were able to provide a more exhaustive series of tests. We also show how the association between paternal incarceration and infant mortality is different for children whose fathers had and had not been abusive to their mothers, allowing for the possibility that paternal incarceration may be protective for—or at least does no significant harm to—some infants.

RESULTS

Figure 5.3 presents some of the key differences between infants who had a parent incarcerated in the last year and those who did not, and also demonstrates some differences not shown in text. It should come as no surprise by now that infants of recently incarcerated parents are at a significant disadvantage relative to infants whose parents did not enter prison or jail. Their mothers were far less likely to be married to their fathers; they were more likely to be African American (not shown); and their mother's experiences during and immediately after the pregnancy were far more stressful than for the other mothers in the sample (not shown).

These infants were also much more likely than other infants to die, although this is somewhat difficult to see in figure 5.3 because we presented the infant mortality rate, which is usually presented per 1,000, as a percentile instead to drive home that few infants do actually die even in this disadvantaged group. Roughly 7 per 1,000 infants of recently incarcerated parents died before the mother was interviewed, as compared to 4 per 1,000 infants whose parents did not experience incarceration recently, an increase of about 75 percent. Infants who experienced parental incarceration also differ from other infants in other ways. Their mothers were dramatically less likely to report having had a previous healthy birth (not shown). The mothers of babies who experienced parental incarceration were also more likely to report smoking and the receipt of public assistance; and, maybe most relevantly, the proportion of them who reported that the father of the child had physically abused them was far greater than in the comparison sample of women in figure 5.3.

As in our analyses in chapters 2, 3, and 4, the children of incarcerated parents are exposed to many other disadvantages at much higher rates than other children before experiencing the incarceration of a parent. They tend to experience multiple disadvantages that accumulate over time and create a host of problems. Viewed this way, parental incarceration is yet another problem to add to

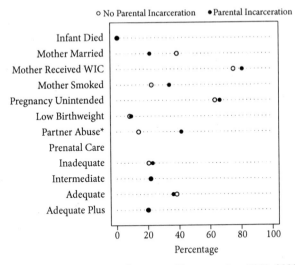

FIGURE 5.3 Descriptive Statistics by Parental Incarceration, 1990–2003

*Information on partner abuse has only been collected since 1995 (N = 42,544).

Notes: All data are weighted. The sample Is limited to women who did not complete high school.

Source: Pregnancy Risk Assessment Monitoring System

an already large pile of difficulties confronting them. This represents a challenge for us, as it makes it difficult to rule out the possibility that our results are driven by the neighborhoods children grow up in, the poverty they face, or the antisocial behaviors their parents engage in. To deal with this difficulty, we employed an array of statistical tests, similar to those we employed in chapter 4 (although, as we mentioned previously, less extensive because of the data limitations we face), designed to make it clear that the associations shown here likely represent harm done by parental incarceration alone.

Figure 5.4 compares models of the odd ratios of infant mortality, after adjusting for a number of background and pregnancy characteristics. (An odds ratio of 100 percent would mean that recent parental incarceration was associated with no change in the

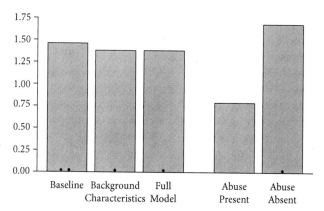

FIGURE 5.4 Early Infant Death by Parental Incarceration and Abuse (Odds Ratios)

Notes: ***p = .001, **p = .01, *p = .1.

Source: Pregnancy Risk Assessment Monitoring System

risk of infant death; so odds ratios greater than 100 percent suggest that recent parental incarceration increases the risk of infant death; and odds ratios less than 100 percent suggest that recent parental incarceration decreases the risk of infant death.) The descriptive model includes simple adjustments for time since birth, state of residence, and year of birth because infant mortality is variable across states and the cumulative risk of mortality increases over the first year of life, although far more infants die in the first hours and days of life than in the subsequent weeks and months. The results suggest there is a basic association between infant mortality and paternal incarceration. In this model, paternal incarceration is associated with a 58 percent increase in the odds of infant death. This is an interesting result, but without adjusting for other confounders, it merely suggests that the relationship is worth investigating further, as it may or may not be due to incarceration.

The demographic model adjusts for basic demographic characteristics and other things that happened prior to the current pregnancy that could also influence the risk of infant mortality (such as having a prior preterm birth). The association between paternal imprisonment and the odds of infant death remains substantial, as recent parental incarceration is associated with a 45 percent increase in the odds of infant mortality. This is roughly comparable in magnitude to the effects of the mother being black ($b = .44$) or Hispanic ($b = -.35$), so given the prominence of maternal race/ethnicity in shaping the risk of infant mortality, it appears that this association is substantial.

The final model (the full model) adjusts for various risk factors having to do with the pregnancy, birth, and immediate aftermath of the birth that have been linked to the risk of infant mortality. Even in this most rigorous model, the association between recent parental incarceration and early infant mortality continues to be statistically significant and substantial, as recent parental incarceration is associated with a 49 percent increase in the odds of early infant mortality. To put the magnitude of this final association in context, consider that it is about as strong as the effects of maternal smoking ($b = .43$) on the risk of infant mortality. Likewise, this association is roughly as important in shaping the risk of infant mortality as is getting adequate prenatal care as opposed to inadequate care ($b = -.46$). Given the voluminous literature on the effects of not only maternal smoking but also quality of prenatal care on the risk of infant mortality, it would be safe to conclude that this association is indeed quite substantial.

Although results show a consistently statistically significant, positive association between recent parental incarceration and infant mortality, as we found for mental health and behavioral problems, the association between parental incarceration and child outcomes may be moderated by whether the father was abusive. Figure 5.4 also compares the effect of paternal incarceration on infant mortality in the presence and absence of abuse by showing the effects separately for the 83 percent of mothers who did not experience abuse and the 17 percent who did. As before, the relationship between parental incarceration and infant mortality is statistically significant (at the .05 level) for women who did not experience abuse. Yet the association increases dramatically, as the odds of early infant mortality are now fully 97 percent higher than the odds for children who did not have a parent incarcerated. The story could hardly be more different for women who had been abused. For these women, having the father of their child incarcerated *decreases* the odds their infants will die in the first year by 17 percent. Unlike the other results shown in figure 5.4, this association is not statistically significant, so we cannot confidently conclude that this protective effect is real (in a statistical sense, at least). But we can certainly conclude that having the father incarcerated doesn't increase the risk of infant mortality for the children of abused mothers.

As in chapter 4, the magnitude of the difference between the effects of paternal incarceration in families where abuse was absent and in families where it was present substantially nuance the findings presented here. At least in the PRAMS data, about 40 percent of recently incarcerated fathers had been reported to have been abusive toward the mother of their children. For these children, just as for childhood mental health and behavioral problems, there is no discernible consequence of recent parental incarceration for early infant mortality. If anything, this event may even *decrease* their risk of infant mortality. For the other 60 percent of the infants, however, parental incarceration is associated with a quite substantial increase in the risk of infant mortality. For these children, holding all else equal, the risk of early infant mortality is about .45 percent; for otherwise comparable children who did not experience recent parental incarceration, the risk is about .23 percent. Thus, parental incarceration is associated with a nearly 100 percent increase in the risk of infant mortality, provided the father did not engage in domestic violence.

CONCLUSION

The results presented thus far suggest that paternal incarceration not only increases the mental health and behavioral problems children exhibit, but also induces calamity in the lives of their families by increasing the risk of infant death. The incarceration of a parent thus not only increases the risks all children contend with, but also increases their risk of an untimely demise.

Importantly, these negative effects are concentrated almost exclusively among infants of fathers who had not been reported to engage in domestic violence. This finding suggests a dilemma for policy makers, a topic we return to when we discuss some policy solutions to these problems in chapter 8. At least in these data, about 40 percent of fathers who had been recently incarcerated were abusive (Figure 5.3). Removing these men from families appears to have little effect on their infant's mortality risk. For the other 60 percent of families, however, paternal incarceration increases the risk of infant mortality, often substantially so.

The size of these effects bears discussion, however, as a clever statistician can make anything sound like a big effect based on statistical significance alone. (Indeed, how can anything that is statistically significant be unimportant substantively?) When researchers who study infant mortality talk about some of the key differences the data show them, they often point to racial differences—as we did in the introduction—or to differences by behaviors detrimental to mother and child alike, such as smoking. After adjusting for all the variables we could muster, parental incarceration increased the odds of infant mortality by about 40 percent in the full sample. To benchmark the size of these effects, consider that African American children had 43 percent higher odds of dying in the first year than white children after adjusting extensively for other traits of their families and environment. That the effects of parental incarceration on infant mortality align with others long studied in the literature in terms of magnitude speaks volumes. To take another example, consider maternal smoking, which is often considered to be one of the most serious (and malleable) risk factors for infant mortality. Maternal smoking increases the odds of infant death by 46 percent, comparable to the parental incarceration effect of 40 percent. That the effects of parental incarceration on infant mortality are as large as the effects of being African

INFANT MORTALITY | 111

American or having a mother who smokes shows just how consequential they are.

These findings, along with studies showing that prison release
may elevate mortality risk in both the short term and the long term
among adult men (Binswanger et al. 2007; Spaulding et al. 2011),
suggest that those weighing the costs and benefits of imprisonment should include another variable in their analysis: years of
life lost for the imprisoned and their family members, including the most vulnerable, their infants. While imprisonment may
save lives by taking dangerous men off the streets, it may also cost
lives by increasing the mortality risks of prisoners and their family members. While increases in the imprisonment rate over the
last thirty-five years have undoubtedly had substantial benefits for
public safety, our analysis of the consequences of parental incarceration for children's subsequent behavior and mental health,
when combined with the findings on infant mortality unearthed
here, suggest that we may have purchased public safety gains at the
expense of the children of the prison boom and a future of greater
inequality.

Of course, saying anything about the long-term consequences
of mass imprisonment for inequality is at this point premature.
Indeed, as provocative as the individual-level analyses shown
in this chapter are, they do not allow us to say anything about
the possible macro-level consequences of mass imprisonment
for the infant mortality rate or racial disparities in the infant
mortality rate. To briefly preview the exercise we undertake in
chapter 7: infant mortality is unique relative to the other outcomes
considered in this book—mental health and behavioral problems
and child homelessness—in that national, state, and local gov-
ernments reliably measure infant mortality rates. Thus, while the
other outcomes we consider here will require us to indirectly test
the consequences of mass imprisonment for black-white inequalities in child well-being, infant mortality allows us to directly test
that relationship by predicting disparities in infant mortality by
imprisonment.

PARENTAL INCARCERATION AND

CHILD HOMELESSNESS

IN CHAPTERS 4 and 5, we detailed the effects of paternal incarceration on childhood mental health and behavioral problems and infant mortality. Here, we describe the effects of paternal incarceration on a final indicator of extreme disadvantage, child homelessness.

Classic accounts of the homeless focus on the single white men who once were the vast majority of this population (Bahr and Caplow 1974); but starting in the early 1980s, the share of the homeless composed of African Americans and children began to grow (Hopper 2003; Lee, Tyler, and Wright 2010: 505). All sorts of statistics illustrate the magnitude of the growing child homelessness problem (and we offer them later in the chapter), but perhaps nothing is more telling than the fact that, in addition to Alex, the Muppet dealing with paternal incarceration, the children's television show *Sesame Street* also introduced a new Muppet character dealing with food insecurity, a key precursor to (and also a consistent consequence of) homelessness.[1]

This shift from a homeless population predominantly composed of old, single, white men to one to which black children increasingly also contribute led to risks of child homelessness that would have been unthinkable before the shift: about 2 percent of American children are homeless each year (National Center on Family Homelessness 2009), with rates approaching 10 percent for African American children living in city centers (Culhane and Metraux 1999: 227–228). Furthermore, as with infant mortality, racial disparities in the risk of child homelessness are striking. According to one analysis, black children ages 0–4 in New York City were between twenty-nine and thirty-five times more likely than white children of the same age to have stayed in a shelter in the last year, a disparity so large that it outpaces nearly every other racial disparity in childhood we can think of (Culhane and Metraux 1999: 227–228).

Like homeless adults, homeless children suffer high rates of victimization (Hagan and McCarthy 1997; Lee, Tyler, and Wright 2010: 506) and exposure to infectious disease (Haddad et al. 2005), have limited access to health care (Kushel, Vittinghoff, and Haas 2001), and are at elevated risk of mortality relative to comparable housed children (Kerker et al. 2011). Furthermore, homeless children struggle to keep up with their schoolwork, are at high risk for abuse, and suffer more mental health problems than other children (Vostanis, Grattan, and Cumella 1997; Buckner 2008; Rafferty, Shinn, and Weitzman 2004). Not surprisingly, child homelessness is also linked to greater food insecurity, worse health, and more difficulty in school (National Center on Family Homelessness 2011), to name just a few of its relevant short-term effects. If the negative effects of homelessness extend into adulthood (and they almost certainly do), child homelessness could imperil well-being throughout the life course and—because of the unequal racial distribution of child homelessness—exacerbate inequality.

Despite its importance and the fact that being homeless as a child is trumped only by one or two more tragic events, such as dying or being placed in foster care because of maltreatment, knowledge about the causes of shifts in the homeless population remains limited. Research shows that changing economic conditions and social policies, deindustrialization, the increasing share of children growing up with a single parent, and the housing squeeze all played a role in these shifts (Hopper 2003; Lee, Tyler, and Wright 2010; Jencks 1994); but little research has considered whether the prison boom played a role. Unfortunately, only one study tests whether parental incarceration increases the risk of child homelessness (Foster and Hagan 2007), and, pathbreaking contribution to research though it is, it uses data that are not well equipped to either decipher whether incarceration causes or correlates with child homelessness or test the mechanisms that might drive children with incarcerated fathers to experience homelessness. Since the micro-foundations upon which claims about the macro-level effects of the prison boom on the homeless population have yet to be rigorously tested, it remains difficult to know whether the prison boom influenced compositional shifts in the homeless population. Absent individual-level estimates of the effects of paternal incarceration on children's risk of being homeless, therefore, it is not possible to gauge whether mass imprisonment shaped racial inequality in child homelessness.

In this chapter, we fill this gap by considering the consequences of paternal incarceration for child homelessness using data from the FFCW study and, in so doing, round out our analysis of the many ways in which paternal incarceration affects individual children. By providing an individual-level test of these relationships, we take a first step toward considering how mass imprisonment could have led to some of the increases in racial inequality in child homelessness since the 1980s. Troubled economic times bring to mind the effects of foreclosure and eviction (Rugh and Massey 2010) on the risk of child homelessness. We argue that the prison boom played a less visible role in the creation of the population of homeless black children even during the widespread economic expansion of the late 1990s.

THE PRISON BOOM AND CHILD HOMELESSNESS

To date, research on the incarceration-homelessness relationship has focused primarily on adult men (Geller and Curtis 2011; Gowan 2002). Although the data used in most of the studies preclude strong statements about causality (but see Geller and Curtis 2011), each study provides insights into the mechanisms leading from incarceration to homelessness. A recent review concluded, "Former inmates wind up with no place to go because of inadequate prerelease preparation, fragile finances, severed social relationships, and barriers posed by their stigmatized identities when seeking employment and housing" (Lee, Tyler, and Wright 2010: 510). Because there are clear mechanisms linking incarceration and homelessness among adult men, a case that this relationship is causal can be made, but research shows that few children endure a bout of homelessness alongside a previously incarcerated father, casting any paternal incarceration-child homelessness relationship in doubt. Indeed, most chronically homeless men become so only after family ties have been severed (Gowan 2002: 508–510), indicating that if paternal incarceration increases children's risk of homelessness, it is unlikely to involve their living with their fathers.

In light of the small proportion of children who will become homeless along with their fathers, we propose a series of *indirect* channels through which having a father incarcerated increases a child's risk of homelessness. In line with what both our discussion of the consequences of paternal incarceration for children's social situations in chapter 3 and research on the causes of child homelessness suggest (Lee, Tyler, and Wright 2010), we expect that paternal incarceration will increase the risk of child homelessness by destabilizing already fragile familial finances, decreasing children's access to institutional and informal supports, and diminishing maternal capacities and capabilities. Although maternal incarceration also likely damages family life in similar ways (Kruttschnitt 2010), we argue that a mother's incarceration only negligibly increases the risk of child homelessness because state interventions push the children of incarcerated mothers into foster care instead (Swann and Sylvester 2006; Johnson and Waldfogel 2004). Thus, paternal and maternal incarceration lead children into different, but parallel, forms of marginalization. While paternal incarceration increases the risk of child homelessness, maternal incarceration increases the risk of foster care placement.

Given the dramatic growth of racial disparity in the risk of parental imprisonment over the last thirty years and the negative effects of paternal incarceration on child homelessness, changes in the American imprisonment rate may have increased the share of the homeless population composed of black children, assuming the effects are either the same size for blacks and whites or are bigger for blacks than whites. As in prevous chapters, we investigate how the effects of paternal incarceration on child homelessness differ by the race of the child. Yet, unlike the analyses presented in those chapters, where black and white children experienced similar effects of having a father incarcerated (the reason we did not discuss race-specific effects in any detail), in this chapter, we find that the effects for black children are far stronger than for other children.

DATA AND METHOD

To test our hypotheses, we used data from the FFCW study. An extensive discussion of these data is available in chapter 4, but since the benefits of these data for this chapter's research question are pronounced, we will linger over them for a moment. These data are uniquely suited to answering our research questions for four reasons. First, they are the only data that are representative of the contemporary children at highest risk of homelessness and contain enough cases of recent paternal incarceration, recent maternal incarceration, and child homelessness to enable us to conduct statistical analyses. Second, because they contain repeated measures of parental incarceration and child homelessness, we are able to establish the appropriate time-ordering between the dependent and explanatory variables. Third, because of the extensive battery of questions about family life included in each wave of the survey, we are able to control for more possible confounders than we could using any prior study in this area, as well as provide compelling tests of the mechanisms that potentially link paternal incarceration and child homelessness. This ability to test mechanisms is especially key because it provides additional insight into the degree to which the factors we think are driving this relationship are or are not doing so. Finally, because many parents in the sample have been incarcerated—including a large number who have been incarcerated recently—these data allow us to more confidently identify causal relationships than we could using a sample in which a smaller percentage of parents had ever been incarcerated (because we can use previously incarcerated fathers as a comparison group of formerly criminally active and criminal justice involved men, as we did in chapter 4).

Whereas in other chapters we have focused exclusively on paternal incarceration, here, we also consider maternal incarceration because we expect the effects of paternal and maternal incarceration to differ. Thus the analyses in the first three figures in the chapter include mothers. In figure 6.1, we take a first step toward considering how parental incarceration influences child homelessness by presenting descriptive differences in homelessness in the last year for children who had a parent incarcerated in the last two-and-a-half years and for those who didn't. Not surprisingly, few children were homeless in the year before the sixty-month FFCW interview. Only about 3 percent of children in this sample had been homeless (not shown), roughly consistent with—if slightly lower than—the yearly risks of homelessness for children living in urban areas found in the most rigorous study to date (Culhane and Meatraux 1999). For children of recently incarcerated fathers, the probability of homelessness was .06; for children not experiencing recent paternal incarceration, the probability was only .02. Differences in the risk for those experiencing and not experiencing recent maternal incarceration were comparable though not statistically significant because of the small sample of incarcerated mothers. At least descriptively, this suggests that both recent paternal incarceration and recent maternal incarceration are associated with substantially elevated risks of child homelessness.

Of course, as we have mentioned many times before, the presence of a strong descriptive relationship between parental incarceration and childhood disadvantage does not mean that parental

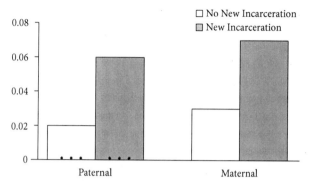

FIGURE 6.1 Recent Homelessness by New Paternal and Maternal Incarceration

Source: Fragile Families & Child Wellbeing Study

incarceration actually caused this event, as these children were likely subject to a whole range of disadvantages before their parents were incarcerated. So, we focus next on some of the differences that are central to shaping these children's risk of being homeless: (1) whether their mother or father had ever been incarcerated before; whether they were (2) living in public housing or (3) receiving cash welfare in the earlier period, and whether they had (4) been homeless or (5) gotten evicted in the previous period. Departing from our earlier analyses, we show these background differences both by recent paternal incarceration and by recent maternal incarceration. But consistent with our previous analyses of the FFCW data, children of recently incarcerated parents would also have been at risk of being homeless for a host of other reasons beyond the factors we focus on here (see especially figures 4.3 and 4.4 in chapter 4).

We consider differences between children with and without recently incarcerated fathers first: figure 6.2 shows pronounced differences in prior paternal incarceration. In our sample, fully 78 percent of recently incarcerated fathers had been incarcerated before, while other fathers were dramatically less likely to have been incarcerated before (although 34 percent of fathers not incarcerated in the last two-and-a-half years having ever been incarcerated before is hardly a negligible amount). These children were also slightly more likely to be living in public housing (20 percent to 15 percent) or to have been recently evicted with their parent at the last wave of data collection (3 percent to 2 percent); and they were far more likely to have their primary caregiver receiving cash welfare at the last data-collection wave (38 percent to 18 percent) or to have been recently homeless (7 percent to 2 percent). Taken together, these differences suggest that the obstacles to causal inference for parental incarceration and child homelessness are especially steep, an important issue for our analysis that we discuss in short order.

Before delving into how we sought to address these obstacles to causal inference, it is worth pointing out, as figure 6.2 does, that the relative level of disadvantage was comparably acute—if not exactly the same—for children of recently incarcerated mothers.

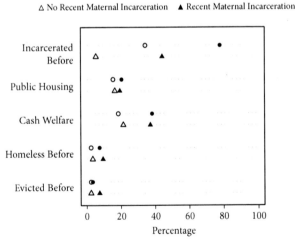

FIGURE 6.2 Descriptive Statistics by Recent Paternal and Maternal Incarceration

Source: Fragile Families & Child Wellbeing Study

As with children of recently incarcerated fathers, recently incarcerated mothers had far more extensive previous involvement with the criminal justice system: fully 44 percent of these mothers compared to only 5 percent of other mothers had been incarcerated before. Also consistent with the situation for recently incarcerated fathers, rates of reliance on public housing (19 percent to 16 percent) and cash welfare (37 percent to 21 percent) were higher, as were rates of prior homelessness (9 percent to 3 percent), and—especially—prior eviction (7 percent to 2 percent). According to these descriptive differences, the children of recently incarcerated mothers seem to be an even more high-risk population than the children of recently incarcerated fathers in some ways.

As in previous chapters, these substantial, preexisting differences between children of recently incarcerated parents and other parents present obstacles to our story. And again, we begin by adjusting for these observed differences, starting with a model that adjusts extensively for key background characteristics (the extended model) and then eventually including prior housing instability (the full model). We then limit the sample to parents who have been criminally active and criminal justice involved before and to children who have never been homeless before in an attempt to show that our results are not driven solely by other stages of criminal justice involvement or affect only children who are so on the margins that they have already been homeless in their first five years of life.

We also present two additional types of tests of the strength and robustness of our relationship. As we did in chapter 4, we present results from matched pairs, including showing how these effects differ for black children and other children, who in our sample are predominantly white and Hispanic. In a final stage, we present what is possibly the most rigorous test presented thus far in the book: we adjust for changes in parental drug/alcohol abuse and in domestic violence in the lead-in to their incarceration. This test is especially important because it lets us confront the hypothesis that what damaged these children's life chances is not a direct effect of incarceration but is instead a time of "fast living," where drinking, drugging, and violence spun out of control and put these children in harm's way. In this final stage, we also provide insight into the degree to which other changes that happened as a result of incarceration—the same mechanisms we discussed earlier—drive this relationship.

RESULTS

Children of recently incarcerated fathers and mothers were four and five percentage points more likely to have been homeless in the last year than children who did not experience this event. On the face of it, this might not seem like much. Yet since this means that children of recently incarcerated parents were roughly three times (6 or 7 percent to 2 percent) more likely to have been homeless, these differences are indeed quite large. What remains to be seen is whether or not having a mother or father incarcerated actually led to this elevated risk of homelessness.

The extended model in figure 6.3 represents our first attempt to see whether this relationship is causal and adjusts for a host of differences between children who do and do not have recently incarcerated parents, including (1) characteristics of the mother and father such as age, education, and race, (2) housing risk factors such as trouble paying bills or receipt of cash welfare, (3) other risk factors such as whether the mother was depressed or how stressed out she was, and (4) prior incarceration. Thus, although this model is but an initial attempt, the adjustments are so extensive that it represents at the very least a level of rigor comparable to the most rigorous research to date on this relationship (Foster and Hagan 2007). Results from the extended model imply that recent paternal incarceration is strongly linked with child homelessness, as the odds ratio of 1.97 indicates, but that recent maternal incarceration is not, as the much lower and statistically insignificant odds ratio of 1.23 for mothers indicates. This difference is virtually identical in the full model, where recent paternal incarceration is linked with

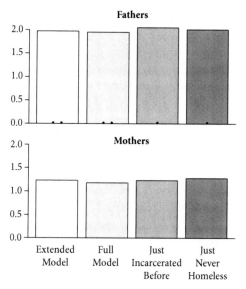

FIGURE 6.3 Results from Logistic Regression Models Predicting Child
Homelessness (Odds Ratios)

Notes: **p <.01, *p <.05

Source: Fragile Families & Child Wellbeing Study

a massive 95 percent increase in the odds of child homelessness,
while recent maternal incarceration is linked with a fairly modest
and statistical insignificant increase of 18 percent.

The final two bars of figure 6.3, which present even more stringent tests by limiting the sample to children of ever-incarcerated
parents or children who have never been homeless before, tells a
similar tale. In each case, recent paternal incarceration is associated with a huge and statistically significant increase in the odds
of child homelessness (105 percent and 101 percent), while recent
maternal incarceration, consistent with the first two bars, is associated with changes in the odds that are simultaneously small
and statistically indistinguishable from zero. Thus, all the results
from figure 6.3 point toward potentially strong effects of recent

paternal—but not maternal—incarceration on children's risk of being homeless in roughly the last year.

Consistent with our hypothesis, our initial analyses suggested that maternal incarceration was unlikely to have any effect on children's risk of homelessness, and so we remove maternal incarceration from the analysis as we move to the more rigorous tests of the relationship between parental incarceration and child homelessness. In figure 6.4, we show how big the differences in the probability of being homeless are based on matching children who are identical in their risk factors for homelessness and only differ on recent paternal incarceration. The first three bars in the figure represent effects based on three different types of matching strategies (described in the methodological appendix). On the basis of each of these three strategies, recent paternal incarceration is linked with about a 2.5 percentage point increase in the risk of child homelessness—ranging from a low of 2.4 percentage points to a high of 2.7 percentage points. This provides further, and even stronger, evidence that recent paternal incarceration increases the homelessness.

Since these effects are also in an easily interpretable metric, unlike odds ratios, which are notoriously difficult to interpret, we linger a minute on just how big these effects are. In figure 6.1, the descriptive difference in the risk of being homeless between children of recently incarcerated fathers and other children was about 4 percentage points—6 percent to 2 percent. In our estimates in figure 6.4, our best guess on how much of that four percentage point difference is due to a causal effect is about 2.5 percentage points. Thus, according to our most stringent test, just over 60 percent of the baseline difference we showed in figure 6.1 appears to be attributable to paternal incarceration.

The implications for inequality of such large effects are likely to be quite consequential. And if they are concentrated among black children, their implications for childhood inequality would be greater still. To consider this possibility, figure 6.4 also presents estimates of the extent to which recent paternal incarceration shapes the risk of child homelessness for black children and for all

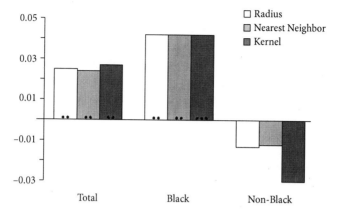

FIGURE 6.4 Estimated Change in the Risk of Experiencing Homelessness Associated with Recent Paternal Incarceration

Notes: ***p = .001, **p = .01, *p = .1.

Source: Fragile Families & Child Wellbeing Study

other children based on matched pairs. Ideally, we would have only included white children in the final group shown in the figure; but because of the small number of observations for white children, we were forced to lump all nonblack children together.

Results from these analyses provide support for two important conclusions. First, and most importantly for high-risk children, paternal incarceration massively increases black children's risk of being homeless, by nearly 5 percentage points in some models. This suggests that the consequences of the prison boom may have been severe for these children. Second, for all other children, however, the relationship actually moves in the other direction, though we must point out that none of these differences are statistically different from zero, so the better interpretation is not that paternal incarceration decreases their risk of child homelessness but that it doesn't do anything to increase it. Based on the results from analyses of matched pairs, therefore, we have even greater evidence that paternal incarceration increases the risk of child homelessness and that it might have dramatically increased black-white inequality in this event.

Yet there is still some work to be done. The skeptic might argue the possibility we noted earlier, that these results are driven by a time of fast living in the lead-in to incarceration (the "fast-living hypotheses") rather than by anything related to the incarceration experience itself. Even though there is no perfect way to address this possibility, and even though this level of skepticism really requires a natural experiment if it persists after tests this rigorous and results this consistent, figure 6.5 presents one way to test this relationship. But this test is somewhat complicated and requires a bit more explanation. The basic idea is this: all our background characteristics are measured when the child is about two-and-a-half years old (or a little bit before); our outcome is measured when the child is about five; and our predictor (recent paternal incarceration) gauges whether the father was incarcerated at any point in between. To test the fast-living hypothesis, we include in our statistical model measures of whether the father developed a drug or alcohol problem or became abusive toward the mother of his child between the child's ages of about two-and-a-half and five. This test, of course, is not perfect, and, as we mentioned a moment ago, skeptics will remain skeptics. Yet when combined with the battery of tests presented elsewhere, it makes a strong case.

But what do the results show? The first bar of figure 6.5 represents the effect of recent paternal incarceration in the full model from figure 6.3 (the second bar there). The second bar of figure 6.5 presents the results from our test of the "fast-living hypothesis." The results thus provide some evidence in favor of our argument and some the skeptic will approve of. When we adjust for changes in drug and alcohol abuse and violence, the relationship does shrink by about one-third (from 1.95 to 1.63), consistent with what the skeptic might argue. Consistent with our argument, however, this effect continues to be large, suggesting that paternal incarceration increases the odds of child homelessness by about 60 percent, and statistically significant. So the results from this analysis suggest that about one-third of the relationship we see here might be due to fast living but that the other two-thirds is likely a causal effect.

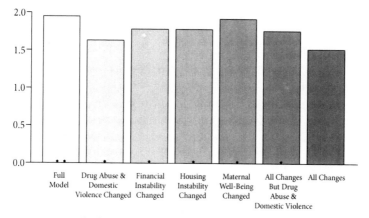

FIGURE 6.5 Results from Logistic Regression Models Considering Mechanisms Linking Recent Paternal Incarceration and Child Homelessness (Odds Ratios)

Notes: **p < .01, *p < 0.5

Source: Fragile Families & Child Wellbeing Study (1998–2005)

Figure 6.5 also serves another purpose: it provides a test of the mechanisms we proposed earlier: destabilizing already fragile familial finances, decreasing children's access to institutional and informal supports, and diminishing maternal capacities and capabilities. Although these results are not strictly about shoring up our causal story, they are nonetheless interesting because they shed light on the degree to which the specific mechanisms we proposed drive the relationship we see here. Based on figure 6.5, it would be safe to conclude that changes in both financial instability and housing instability explain about 20 percent of the observed relationship, which doesn't sound like much but is pretty good by social scientific standards. Changes in maternal capacities, on the other hand, explain almost none of the relationship, suggesting that mothers who suffer declines in their mental health as a result of their partner's incarceration may find a way to buffer their children from homelessness, even if they cannot do the same for the negative effects of financial and housing insecurity. The final two bars of figure 6.5, which include all the mechanisms that we speculated drive this relationship, except fast living (bar one) and including fast living (bar two), imply that adjusting for all mechanisms alone explains, again, 20 percent of the relationship, and that also taking fast living into account explains nearly half of the relationship discussed in this chapter. Thus, although we cannot fully account statistically for what drives this relationship, we can account for roughly half of the statistical relationship identified in this chapter.

CONCLUSION

Using data uniquely suited to the consideration of these research questions, we show that recent paternal incarceration increases the risk of child homelessness. As with mental health and behavioral problems and infant mortality, the association between paternal incarceration and homelessness is robust across several modeling strategies. Furthermore, the magnitude of these effects was large. The estimated effects of recent paternal incarceration on the risk of child homelessness ranged from 2.4 percentage points to 2.7 percentage points in the most rigorous models we employed (figure 6.4). These effects, moreover, stood up not only to limiting the sample to those who had already been incarcerated before (figure 6.3), but also to including an especially rigorous test of the "fast-living hypothesis" (figure 6.5), which presents an especially serious threat to causal inference. The effects of recent paternal incarceration on child homelessness, moreover, were concentrated almost exclusively among black children. Examining the reasons for this finding is beyond the scope of this book, but the implications of the finding are not because this concentration of effects suggests large effects on inequality.

Although the results suggested a robust relationship between recent paternal incarceration and child homelessness, they did not suggest that recent maternal incarceration had a significant effect on the risk of child homelessness. The relationship between recent maternal incarceration and child homelessness was always positive, but the coefficients were generally about one-third as large as coefficients for recent paternal incarceration and never approached significance. Extant research suggests that children of incarcerated mothers are at greater risk of foster care placement relative to homelessness, and our results confirm this. Thus, the results suggest that changes in female imprisonment rates did not play a key role in the increasing risk of child homelessness in recent decades, whereas changes in the male imprisonment rate likely did.

These results thus have a number of implications for how we think about the American systems of imprisonment, stratification, and marginalization. Perhaps most importantly, the results indicate that paternal and maternal incarceration lead to parallel paths of marginalization for children. While the effects of maternal incarceration on children's risk of foster care placement have been well-documented (Swann and Sylvester 2006), this chapter is the first to show that recent paternal but not maternal incarceration increases the risk of child homelessness. Second, the substantial effects of recent paternal incarceration on the risk of child homelessness have important implications at the macro-level— especially since these estimates were culled from the strongest empirical test in this area to date. When these negative effects are combined with massive increases and racial disparity in the risk of paternal imprisonment since the early 1980s, they imply that the prison boom may have played a role in the increasing risk of homelessness for American children over this period—and that the effects on the risk of homelessness for black children may have been especially profound since they are more likely to experience parental imprisonment and more likely to become homeless as a result of that event. Thus, while economic downturns trigger concern about housing instability (Rugh and Massey 2010), the prison boom may have played a silent but vital role in the increasing risk of homelessness for American children even when the economy was healthy. The results presented here highlight the prison boom as a potentially important cause of racial inequality in child homelessness. Of course, to know how large the effects of mass imprisonment on racial inequality in child homelessness are, we need to consider inequality, an exercise we undertake in chapter 7.

MASS IMPRISONMENT AND

CHILDHOOD INEQUALITY

WE HAVE SHOWN that having a father imprisoned has become an alarmingly common experience in the life course for marginalized children. According to our estimates, one in four of today's African American young adults had their father imprisoned at some point. For those whose fathers did not graduate from high school, one in two experienced parental imprisonment. Yet, if paternal imprisonment does not harm children, merely signaling disadvantage or even helping at-risk children, then the consequences for inequality of this sea change in the risk of parental imprisonment would be small. In the previous three chapters, we used a range of different statistical methods and three different data sets to show that paternal imprisonment does serious harm to children. Indeed, our results suggest that having a father incarcerated increases children's mental health and behavioral problems, risk of being homeless, and even the chance that they will die before they complete their first year of life. All three outcomes suggest that the children of ever-imprisoned fathers are a group at extremely high risk for troubled transitions to adulthood—in no small part because of the penal system. Yet, the goal of this book is neither to simply document black-white disparities in the cumulative risk of parental imprisonment nor to show how negative the individual-level consequences of having a father incarcerated are for children in a number of different domains. Our goal is to consider the consequences of mass imprisonment for inequality among children.

This task, it turns out, is new to research on the effects of mass imprisonment on children. Furthermore, the available evidence—from research on the consequences of mass imprisonment for inequality among adults—provides divergent perspectives based on the outcome considered and the method used. Combining individual-level effects of imprisonment on men's earnings with disparities in risks of imprisonment, Western (2006:127) estimates that mass imprisonment has increased black-white disparities in lifetime earnings by just 3 percent. Similar methods show only small changes in the chance of ever marrying (Lopoo and Western 2005: 730). To the contrary, using macro-level data, Johnson and Raphael (2009) estimate that most of the black-white disparity in AIDS cases is attributable to changes in the American imprisonment rate. So, how large are the effects of mass imprisonment on childhood inequality? Has mass imprisonment had a small effect, as with black-white disparities in the lifetime earnings or the chance of marrying for men, or has it had a massive effect, as with black-white disparities in AIDS?

ESTIMATING EFFECTS OF MASS IMPRISONMENT ON INEQUALITY

There are two ways in which researchers interested in mass imprisonment have estimated effects of mass imprisonment on inequality: (1) combining individual-level effects of imprisonment with disparities in the lifetime risk of imprisonment, and (2) using macro-level data to directly test the effects on inequality of changes in the imprisonment rate. Each one has benefits and drawbacks.

The first of these methods is a natural extension of the analyses we have presented to this point. It has three stages. First, we consider what black-white differences in a given outcome—mental health and behavioral problems, homelessness, or infant mortality—would be if no children experienced parental incarceration. The simplest way to do this, which we adopt here, is to compare outcomes for black children and white children who do not experience parental incarceration. This necessarily provides us with a rough estimate of how large the gaps would be. It also provides a good starting point for thinking about inequality. An added benefit is that it almost certainly *underestimates* what inequality would be absent incarceration because a smaller share of disadvantaged white children than black children are excluded from the comparison. Next, we estimate effects of parental incarceration on the outcome across a range of models to get a sense of what the average effect across various models could be. This is what we did in chapters 4, 5 and 6, where we were trying to identify effects. Third, and finally, we combine these effects with the percentage of black children and of white children who will likely experience paternal incarceration under various incarceration levels—in this analysis, we use the risks of paternal incarceration for the 1978 and 1990 birth cohorts described in chapter 2. Once this stage is completed, we can estimate how much greater the black-white gap in all of the outcomes we consider here is because of changes in the American imprisonment rate.

There are many benefits to using this method. Perhaps most importantly, it combines estimates of the causal effects and social patterning of the risk of paternal imprisonment that we calculated using the highest-quality data. We can also use it for any outcome, provided we can estimate its individual-level causal effects. Yet, despite these two main benefits, there are a number of difficulties with this method. On the most basic level, it only allows us to consider the *direct* effects of changes in the level of paternal incarceration on inequality among children. This is problematic because if the indirect effects of imprisonment help children, as research on the crime-fighting benefits of imprisonment (Johnson and Raphael 2012) and the harmful effects of crime on child well-being (Sharkey 2010) suggest, we will overestimate effects on inequality by not incorporating them into our calculation (Sampson 2011). On the other hand, if the indirect effects of imprisonment harm children, as research on the corrosive effects of high imprisonment rates in low-income communities (Clear 2007) and poor schools (Hagan and Foster 2012) suggest, then we are underestimating effects on inequality. It is therefore difficult to know using this method whether we are overestimating or underestimating the effects of mass imprisonment on inequality among children. It is also somewhat troubling, though certainly less so, that the samples we use to estimate causal effects tend to not be nationally representative—representing instead a large subset of children, as in the FFCW, PHDCN, and PRAMS data—and yield estimates of the effects of parental *incarceration* rather than *imprisonment* when, at the same time, our estimates of racial disparities in the social patterning of this risk include only prison incarceration. These are important caveats, and the estimates we present here should not be thought of as perfectly accurate point estimates. That said, there is little reason to think that they represent large overestimates of the inequality caused by paternal incarceration. More importantly, as we describe in detail later, the magnitude and consistency of the estimates we present here preclude any reasonable argument that paternal imprisonment has decreased (or has no effect on) inequality among children.

The second method for estimating the effects of imprisonment on black-white inequality among children involves using complex statistical techniques to directly estimate effects using macro-level data—usually state-level data. Rather than multiple stages, this method simply involves estimating causal effects of changes in the imprisonment rate on some outcome and then estimating how different black-white inequality would be at different levels of imprisonment. This method is desirable because it attempts to estimate a total effect that includes both the direct and indirect effects of imprisonment. Yet, it also has some severe limitations, including that it is difficult to tell whether direct or indirect effects are driving any relationship, and it can only be utilized when the outcome for both blacks and whites has been measured over a long period. This, it turns out, poses a major problem for researchers since just one of the child outcomes we consider—the infant mortality rate—has been measured consistently at the state-level by race for a long time.

It is possible to unite the individual-level estimates of causal effects and the cumulative risk of paternal imprisonment for nearly any outcome, yet this assumes that all mass-imprisonment consequences on childhood inequality are direct. Relying solely on macro-level data to consider these relationships incorporates both direct and indirect effects, but it is more difficult to tell whether the relationship being isolated is actually causal, and the method can be used only when the outcome of interest is measured at the state-level, which is quite rare, unfortunately. What to do? In light of the limitations of each method, we propose using both whenever possible—as we did with the infant mortality rate in this analysis—and relying on whichever method has the most appropriate data when both types of tests cannot be conducted, as was the case with our other outcomes, where we have excellent individual-level data and virtually no state-level data.

EFFECTS ON INEQUALITY USING MICRO-LEVEL DATA

Establishing Baseline Levels of Inequality

The first stage in considering the effects of mass imprisonment on inequalities in child well-being is to establish baseline levels of inequality for each outcome we consider. There are many ways to estimate such differences, and each has pros and cons. We opt to compare black children and white children who did not experience paternal incarceration in the PHDCN, FFCW, and PRAMS data sets because this provides us with conservative estimates of how large the black-white disparities would be absent parental incarceration.

Figures 7.1 and 7.2 display these differences for all the outcomes we considered in chapters 4, 5, and 6. Even absent parental incarceration, black-white disparities in childhood mental health and behavioral problems would have been substantial.

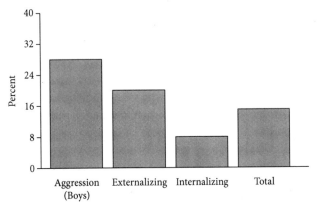

FIGURE 7.1 Black-White Disparities in Mental Health and Behavioral Problems Absent Paternal Incarceration

Source: Project on Human Development in Chicago Neighborhoods and Fragile Families & Child Wellbeing Study

Analyses of the PHDCN data show that black children exhibited 8 percent higher levels of internalizing behaviors, 20 percent higher levels of externalizing behaviors, and 15 percent higher levels of total behavioral problems. Based on analyses of the FFCW data, our results suggest that black boys would be 29 percent more physically aggressive than white boys absent parental incarceration.

If baseline differences in behavioral problems between black children and white children suggest that mass imprisonment is not the sole force contributing to racial disparities, this is even more true of severe forms of childhood disadvantage such as infant mortality and child homelessness. Even absent parental incarceration, results using the PRAMS data suggest that black infants were 138 percent more likely to die in their first year than white infants. Differences were even more notable for child homelessness; the FFCW data indicate that black children were 144 percent more likely than white children to have been homeless in the last year absent incarceration.

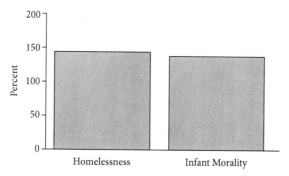

FIGURE 7.2 Black-White Disparities in Homelessness and Infant Mortality Absent Paternal Incarceration

Source: Fragile Families & Child Wellbeing Study and Pregnancy Risk Assessment Monitoring System

How Much Paternal Incarceration Increases These Risks

Taken together, our analyses of the PHDCN, FFCW, and PRAMS data sets suggest that absent changes in the American imprisonment rate since the mid-1970s, racial disparities in children's mental health and behavioral problems, as well as their risks of infant mortality and child homelessness, would still have been quite substantial. Nonetheless, if parental incarceration harms children, as we now know it does, and is highly unequally distributed, as we now know it is, then mass imprisonment can exacerbate these disparities. To know how much it could increase black-white disparities, we first need to know what percentage change in each problem paternal incarceration causes for the individual children who experience it.

We display this information in figure 7.3. To again start with children's behavioral and mental health problems, our highest and lowest estimates based on various modeling strategies show that paternal incarceration increases children's internalizing behavioral problems between 5 percent and 6 percent, externalizing behavioral

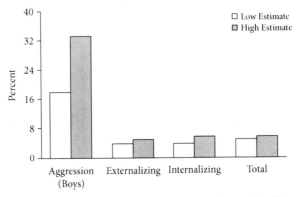

FIGURE 7.3 Percent Increase in Mental Health and Behavioral Problems due to Paternal Incarceration

Source: Project on Human Development in Chicago Neighborhoods and Fragile Families & Child Wellbeing Study

problems between 4 percent and 6 percent, and total behavioral problems between 4 percent and 5 percent. The consequences for boys' physically aggressive behaviors were far more pronounced, with the smallest estimated effect (18 percent) being triple those estimated for the broader range of behavioral problems and the largest estimated effect (33 percent) six times the size of those estimated earlier. This is especially noteworthy since the largest baseline black-white differences in behavioral and mental health problems were also found for the physical aggression of boys, suggesting that the prison boom may have contributed to already substantial racial disparities in boys' physical aggression, with potential implications for the future of the criminal justice system, a possibility rarely grappled with in the research on the prison boom.

The magnitude of the effects was far greater for severe forms of disadvantage. For the infant mortality rate, estimated effects suggested that parental incarceration increased that risk by 47 percent to 49 percent.[1] For child homelessness, effects were even more substantial, increasing the risk of experiencing that event by 94 percent to 99 percent. Aside from the fact that this is far and away the

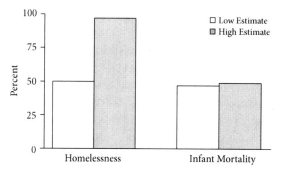

FIGURE 7.4 Percent Increase in Risks of Homelessness and Infant Mortality due to Paternal Incarceration

Source: Fragile Families & Child Wellbeing Study and Pregnancy Risk Assessment Monitoring System

largest percent increase associated with paternal incarceration, child homelessness is also interesting because it is the sole case in which differences in the effects for whites and blacks differed significantly and consistently. According to estimates presented in chapter 6, paternal incarceration is associated with a 15 percent to 18 percent *decrease* in the risk of homelessness for white children, whereas it is associated with a 138 percent to 140 percent *increase* in that same risk for black children. Given the magnitude of these effects and the fact that they are almost exclusively concentrated among black children, the effects of mass imprisonment on black-white disparities in the risk of child homelessness may be far larger than for the other outcomes we consider, a possibility we ignored in our initial inequality estimates but revised for our final estimates.

Incorporating Disparities in Cumulative Risks of Paternal Imprisonment

To estimate the effects of mass imprisonment on black-white disparities in child well-being, we need to know not only how large the effects of paternal incarceration are for individual children but also how unequally distributed the risk of experiencing these events is by race. We presented these estimates in greater detail in chapter 2, so we merely review the key findings here. According to our estimates, white children born in 1978 had about a 1.4 percent chance of experiencing paternal imprisonment. For black children born that same year, the risk was 13.8 percent. For white children born in 1990, the cumulative risk was 3.3 percent. For black children born that same year, the risk of paternal imprisonment was 25.1 percent. In estimating effects on childhood inequality, we multiply the estimated effects of paternal incarceration on individual children by the percentage of children experiencing that event. Doing that for each race-cohort allows us to see how much mass imprisonment shaped childhood inequality.

Mass Imprisonment and the Growth in Childhood Inequality

In figure 7.5, we present estimates of how much black-white inequality in child behavioral and mental health problems, child homelessness, and infant mortality would have increased if the cumulative risk of paternal imprisonment had increased from zero to the 1978 and 1990 levels. In so doing, we provide the first estimates of how much mass imprisonment might exacerbate inequality not only in the contemporary era, but also long into the future.

To start with behavioral and mental health problems, our estimates suggest that the consequences of mass imprisonment for black-white disparities in total behavioral problems have been fairly small, increasing them around 5 percent for children born in 1978 and only about 10 percent for children born in 1990. For total behavioral problems, therefore, the effects of mass imprisonment on childhood inequality are only somewhat more pronounced than its effects on black-white inequalities in lifetime earnings among adult men. They are quite small.

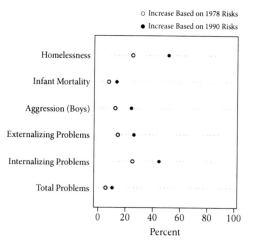

FIGURE 7.5 Initial Estimates of Increase in Black-White Disparities in Child Wellbeing due to Incarceration

Source: Authors' calculations

The same cannot be said for other types of behavioral problems. Our estimates suggest that racial disparities in internalizing behaviors were 25 percent higher for children born in 1978 than would have been expected under zero incarceration and 46 percent higher for children born in 1990. Effects on black-white gaps in externalizing behaviors for all children (14 percent for 1978, 26 percent for 1990) and physical aggression for boys (13 percent for 1978, 24 percent for 1990) were somewhat smaller than they were for internalizing behaviors but still substantial and much larger than effects for total behavioral problems. Indeed, these results suggest that even based on the 1978 estimate, which is far too low for contemporary children, the effects of mass imprisonment on childhood inequality in behavioral problems would have been between four and six times the size of the effects that Western (2006) showed for inequality in men's earnings.

Effects on inequality in more severe forms of childhood disadvantage are also sometimes substantial. For the infant mortality rate, however, they are not overwhelmingly large. According to our estimates using only micro-level data, the black-white gap in the infant mortality rate was only 7 percent larger for children born in 1978 than it would have been under zero incarceration. And even based on 1990 levels of paternal imprisonment, the rate would be only 13 percent more than predicted under zero incarceration. These effects on black-white inequality are fairly small in that they line up more with effects on total behavioral problems than internalizing or externalizing behavioral problems, where we saw large effects. Effects on black-white inequality in child homelessness are more pronounced. Assuming uniform effects of paternal incarceration on black and white children, as we do in our initial estimates shown in figure 7.5, our estimates show that the black-white gap in child homelessness would have been 25 percent greater for children born in 1978 than under zero incarceration and fully 52 percent greater for children born in 1990. Since the effects of child homelessness were heavily concentrated among black children, if we allow the effects of paternal incarceration on children to vary, as we do later, we see even more substantial effects on inequality. According to these estimates, black-white gaps in child homelessness would have been about 38 percent (for children born in 1978) to 65 percent (for children born in 1990) greater than for children born under zero incarceration.

EFFECTS ON INEQUALITY USING MACRO-LEVEL DATA

The first stage of our analysis estimated macro-level effects on childhood inequality using a combination of micro-level estimates of causal effects on a range of outcomes and the changing social patterning of paternal imprisonment. This showed effects on black-white inequality ranging from a 5 percent to 10 percent increase (for total behavioral problems) to a 25 percent to 52 percent increase (for child homelessness, assuming uniform effects of paternal incarceration on child homelessness by race), with effects on black-white inequalities in the other outcomes considered—internalizing, externalizing, and physically aggressive behaviors, as well as infant mortality—falling somewhere in between. Unfortunately, the methods we utilized did not let us consider both the direct and indirect effects of incarceration on inequality, which is problematic since research in this area suggests that indirect effects of incarceration can help (Sampson 2011; Sharkey 2010) or harm child well-being (Clear 2007).

Using the second method described above for estimating direct and indirect effects, figure 7.6 describes the direct and indirect contributions attributable to parental incarceration for inequality in infant mortality rates. Rather than using multiple stages, as the first method did, we directly estimate the influence of incarceration on infant mortality rates using state-level data. After producing an estimate, we simply apply different levels of incarceration to the effect as we did above, tracking how much black-white inequality in infant mortality rates change with increasing incarceration rates. By considering effects on black-white disparities in the infant mortality rate using both of the methods described

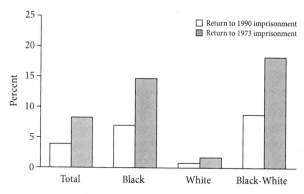

FIGURE 7.6 Decrease in Infant Mortality Rates at Lower Imprisonment Rates, State-Level Analysis

Source: Authors' calculations

above, we show how incorporating or failing to incorporate spill-over effects changes our inequality estimates. We focus only on the infant mortality rate because none of the other outcomes we considered have been measured well enough at the macro-level to estimate effects. Because we directly estimate effects on inequality in this stage of the analysis, this stage is more involved and is described in the methodological appendix.[2]

According to the estimates for the total infant mortality rates, had the imprisonment rate remained at the 1990 level, the infant mortality rate would have been 3.9 percent lower. Had it remained instead at the 1973 level, the infant mortality rate would have been 8.3 percent lower, which corresponds with roughly one additional death per 2,000 live births in the United States over this period, a seemingly small but actually large effect. The direct and indirect effects of paternal incarceration on infant mortality rates are large indeed—there is a positive, substantial, significant association between the imprisonment rate and the total infant mortality rate.

Knowing how the imprisonment rate is associated with the total infant mortality is crucial, but our end goal is to know how it associates with the black and white infant mortality rates so we can find out how it changes inequality in them. According to our estimates, had the imprisonment rate remained at the 1990 level, the black infant mortality rate would have been 7 percent lower. Had it remained at the 1973 level, it would have been 14.7 percent lower. Increased imprisonment had a profound effect on the black infant mortality rate, but results for the white infant mortality rate could hardly differ more. The associations between the imprisonment rate and the white infant mortality rate are neither statistically significant nor substantial.[3] Given how small this association is and how large the association of imprisonment with the black infant mortality is, it is unsurprising that imprisonment is significantly and positively associated with the absolute black-white disparity in the infant mortality rate.

The macro-level consequences of mass imprisonment for the black-white gap in the infant mortality rate are substantial. The black-white gap in the infant mortality rate would have been 8.8 percent lower had the imprisonment rate remained at the 1990 level, and a startling 18.3 percent lower had it remained at the 1973 level. This corresponds to about a 1.5 (to 2.0) per 1,000 decrease in the black-white gap in the infant mortality rate. In models shown in the methodological appendix, we find that each one standard deviation increase in the imprisonment rate is associated with a .34 standard deviation increase in the absolute black-white disparity in the infant mortality rate. To put the magnitude of this coefficient into another perspective, the imprisonment-infant mortality relationship is large in comparison to other important factors affecting health, public safety, and well-being. The imprisonment rate is almost as strongly associated with the infant mortality rate (.25) as the violent crime rate (.33), for example.

Interestingly, the macro-level models show somewhat larger differences on racial disparities in the infant mortality rate than the micro-level stage of the analysis did. According to our estimates culled using micro-level data, black-white inequality in the infant mortality rate would have been 7 percent to 13 percent lower absent incarceration. Yet according to our macro-level analysis, the black-white disparity in the infant mortality rate would have been slightly higher, at 9 percent to 18 percent greater absent increases in incarceration. Of course, the baselines for these two analyses do not line up perfectly, so not too much should be made of these differences. But it is reassuring that the estimated effects line up fairly well using disparate methods. And, as figure 7.7, which also allows the effect of paternal incarceration on child homelessness to vary by the race of the child, shows, our final estimates of the effects of mass imprisonment on black-white disparities in child well-being are somewhat larger than our initial estimates shown in figure 7.5.

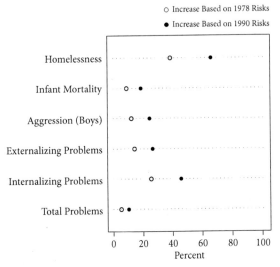

FIGURE 7.7 Final Estimates of Increase in Black-White Disparities in Child Well-Being due to Incarceration

Source: Authors' calculations

CONCLUSION

Of all the findings on the research on the consequences of mass imprisonment, maybe the most perplexing has to do with its consequences for black-white inequality among adult men. As the prison boom took hold, the experience of imprisonment became shockingly common for black adult men. Depending on the estimate considered, somewhere between 20 percent and 25 percent of black men can now expect to experience imprisonment by their early thirties, and far more will experience it at some point during their lives (Western and Wildeman 2009; Bonczar 2003; Pettit and Western 2004). The experience, furthermore, has been shown to have substantial negative effects on their subsequent well-being in a host of domains, especially in terms of their earnings and risk of divorce (Western 2006, 2002; Massoglia, Remster, and King 2011;

Lopoo and Western 2005). Given the highly unequal distribution of the experience of imprisonment and these negative effects, it is reasonable to assume that mass imprisonment has led to substantial growth in the black-white disparities in a host of domains. Yet, with the exception of black-white disparities in AIDS infection rates (Johnson and Raphael 2009), existing research suggests that mass imprisonment has done little to exacerbate inequality among adult men, as mass incarceration increased black-white disparities in men's lifetime earnings 3 percent (Western 2006) and marriage 4 percent (Lopoo and Western 2005).

Our goal has been to consider whether mass imprisonment has also had small effects on black-white inequality among children. Chapter 2 showed that the risk of paternal imprisonment has increased in lockstep with the lifetime risks of imprisonment for adult men, suggesting that paternal imprisonment is now sufficiently unequally distributed to have important effects on inequality, provided paternal incarceration harms children. Chapters 4, 5, and 6 suggested that paternal incarceration does indeed do substantial harm to children—even if it does not dramatically harm children of abusive fathers. Yet, as we saw for adult men, the combination of negative individual-level effects and unequal risks does not guarantee large effects on inequality. Indeed, we might expect fairly small effects on childhood inequality in light of the fairly small effects that previous research shows for inequality among adult men.

Our inequality estimates are quite contrary to those estimated for adult men. Figure 7.7 summarizes them across all the outcomes that we have considered here. Our analyses suggest small effects on some outcomes, such as total behavioral problems, where mass incarceration is associated with a 5 percent to 10 percent increase in black-white inequality. Yet for other outcomes, such as child homelessness, we see much more pronounced effects; here, mass incarceration is associated with about a 65 percent increase in the already large black-white disparities in the risk of child homelessness. Effects on inequalities in other domains, from infant mortality to internalizing, externalizing, and physical aggression fall somewhere in between. But in each case, the effects on black-white disparities in childhood inequality were far greater than the effects on adult inequality.

These findings, as we discuss in greater detail in chapter 8, suggest that the largest effects of mass imprisonment on social inequality may be yet to come—even if the imprisonment rate were to return to a moderate level in short order. Indeed, given the large effects we found on inequality in the behavioral and mental health problems that so profoundly shape children's future life chances, we might expect mass imprisonment to contribute to inequality among the children of the prison boom, not just while they are children, but also as they age into adolescence and even adulthood. Results for inequality in the infant mortality rate and child homelessness, furthermore, suggest that mass imprisonment may also have large effects on inequality in the racial distribution of the most disadvantaged children. In an era in which it is hoped that blacks and whites have increasingly open channels to quality of life, this finding is perhaps all the more disheartening since it portends the creation of a new underclass.

CONCLUSION

When we think of things that affect children's well-being and development, we tend to think of our own childhoods and how they shaped our lives. We might think of significant events in family life, like our parents splitting up or remarrying, and how they affected us emotionally or financially. Likewise, our thoughts might transport us back to the neighborhood we grew up in and how its characteristics—proximity to friends, the park in the center of the neighborhood, or the one especially dangerous street corner—shaped us. Some of us might remember uniquely stressful times that lasted much longer than we anticipated—a parent's umployment, the unsteady months as the bills piled up, and arguments between our parents that flared up with little warning as a result of the stress. We might think about the elementary school we attended and how it shaped our development, identity, and social network. Indeed, most of us have a sense of how good (or not) the schools we attended were and memories of an exceptionally helpful (or unhelpful) teacher who influenced our intellectual development—or at least our grades.

For those of us now in our thirties, our experiences in these four contexts—the structure of our families, the neighborhoods we grew up in, the stressors our families faced, and the schools we went to—profoundly shaped our perceptions of the differences between us and the other kids we grew up with. Indeed, most of us have a childhood friend whose trajectory diverged from ours (for better or worse) because of differences in family structure, neighborhood and school contexts, or stressful life experiences. And many of us can probably remember distinctly how our trajectory diverged from that of a friend who attended the fancy private school instead of our neighborhood school, whose parents went through a lengthy and acrimonious divorce, who grew up on the wrong side of the tracks, or whose parents inherited a great deal of money.

CHILDREN OF THE PRISON BOOM

Yet for children growing up even just ten or fifteen years after we did, who were born in the early 1990s, like Michael and Nathaniel whose stories we told in the introduction, a new childhood experience can be added to the list: whether a parent went to prison at some point in their childhood. As we showed in chapter 2, the changes in the risk of paternal imprisonment between the 1978 and 1990 birth cohorts—the thirty-five-year-olds and twenty-three-year-olds of today—were dramatic; so were those for maternal imprisonment, albeit to a lesser degree. Parental imprisonment was transformed from an event affecting only the unluckiest of children—children of parents whose involvement in crime was quite extensive or extremely serious—to one that was remarkably common for black children. According to our estimates, about one in four of the black twenty-three-year-olds of today had a parent imprisoned at some point in his or her childhood. For the same generation of children whose fathers dropped out of high school, about one in two had a father imprisoned at some point, according to our calculations. The prolonged absence of a father due to imprisonment has become common for recent generations of black children—especially those whose fathers dropped out of high school. Indeed, as we have argued throughout the book, we can no longer ignore the relevance of the penal system for black children born in the last twenty years.

If parental imprisonment is such a common experience for black children and children whose parents dropped out of high school, why do we know so little about it? In many ways, it is surprising that a book on this topic seems new given the stark findings on the dramatic increases in the risk of paternal imprisonment since the late 1970s. Several early and groundbreaking qualitative works highlighted the potential importance of parental imprisonment (e.g., Arditti 2012; Foster and Hagan 2007; Gabel and Johnston 1998; Murray and Farrington 2005; Nurse 2002; Sack 1977; Siegel 2011); but few of them explicitly addressed growing inequality among children, and most were based on data that did not allow researchers to adequately correct for selection bias—at least not in the way quantitative researchers tend to want to do. Beyond these seminal works, scholarly work on parental incarceration in sociology, psychology, and criminology was notably absent well into the prison boom.

We think that some of the reason for this inattention is precisely that parental incarceration remains so uncommon for white children. Considering a comparison case might be useful here. Despite the current widespread interest in divorce within the research community, few studies considered the effects of divorce on child well-being and development until it became common among highly educated whites (Cherlin 1999). As the results from chapter 2 suggest, growth in the risk of paternal imprisonment for white children has just not been that extreme. Even for white children born in 1990, the risk of paternal imprisonment was still only about 1 in 30—a number not even in the same ballpark as the risk for black children born in the same year. Furthermore, for white children of fathers who had some college education—not just those who completed their degree—the risk of ever having a father imprisoned is about 1 in 100. To put this risk in context, consider that the risk of dying before age fourteen is also roughly 1 in 100 for white children born in 1990, showing just how uncommon paternal incarceration is among white children (US Department of Health and Human Services 1994).

THE FUTURE OF INEQUALITY IN AMERICA

Regardless of why the tremendous growth in the risk of paternal imprisonment for black children received relatively little attention until very recently, the stark comparison between the cumulative risks of paternal imprisonment for black children (25.1 percent) and white children (3.6 percent) suggest that paternal imprisonment can exacerbate racial inequalities in children's well-being and development—if it has negative effects on children. Of course, this is quite a big *if*, and we spent all of chapter 3 discussing the various reasons that we should expect paternal imprisonment to harm children. The gut feeling of many people is that having a parent go to prison should be good for children. Indeed, the removal of a potentially disruptive, impulsive, selfish, violent, drug-addicted, and criminally active parent should help children, shouldn't it? Although we agree that in the most extreme circumstances the removal of parents enhances child well-being, we showed in chapter 3 that most inmate parents just don't seem nearly as bad as some might expect. Many of them struggle with addiction, have trouble holding down a job or finding safe, stable housing, have low levels of educational attainment, and struggle with some (fairly mild) mental illnesses, such as depression, to be sure. But very few fit the profile of the violent, pathological individual who actively does harm to his children. So, although the average inmate father has his struggles, they are not the struggles popular images of prison inmates suggest. Indeed, as with mothers trying to make ends meet, the portrait of inmate fathers is more one of crushing poverty and a lifetime of disadvantages than of a psychopath.

In most instances, the removal of the parent makes a bad situation worse, a theme we return to again and again in our analyses in chapters 3, 4, 5, and 6. On the one hand, this claim is bolstered by statistical evidence presented in chapter 3 showing the incarceration of a father to be linked with broad changes in family life, nearly all of which were linked with harm. On the other hand, the qualitative interviews presented there showed the rich texture of how the incarceration of a father harms children, even if it does so in a complex manner. The qualitative data also make something else clear: even if the *average* effects of paternal incarceration on children are likely to be negative, the experience may be protective for some. Especially for children subjected to physical, sexual, or emotional abuse by the parent who is removed, incarceration might even provide some a brief respite.

Given what we know about changes in the type of criminals who have been drawn into prisons between the early 1970s and the early 2010s, this should not come as a great surprise. Prisons used to be reserved for the most heinous or persistent offenders. Now they are also reserved for the intermittently homeless, those who struggle with mental illnesses and addictions, and the chronically poor. Of course, individuals who are chronically poor, struggle with mental illnesses and addiction, and are sometimes homeless face many stressors that can make parenting difficult. Yet, given what we now know about the effects of parents on children, having these parents removed because of incarceration likely does more harm than good. It would certainly be better for children for their parents not to be criminally active, poor, struggling with addiction or mental illness, or unable to secure stable housing; but the best research simply does not suggest that removing this parent from the child's life would benefit them. In statistical parlance, the reference cell should be a parent who is not struggling with all these things rather than not having a parent at all.

Having a theoretical framework suggesting that parental imprisonment will harm children is not the same thing as having evidence that it actually does, however. In chapters 4, 5, and 6, we rigorously tested the effects of paternal incarceration on children using the best available data, focusing on two very different types of outcomes. In chapter 4, we focused on children's behavioral and mental health problems using the best available data—the Project on Human Development in Chicago Neighborhoods and the Fragile Families and Child Wellbeing study. These behaviors are interesting, not just because nearly all parents can remember a time when their children withdrew, acted out, or lashed out in response to the trauma of moving to a new city, changing schools, or having a parent move out, but also because of how well they predict the subsequent problems in adolescence and adulthood. Indeed, childhood behavioral problems are some of the strongest predictors of adjustment in a host of key domains ranging from criminal activity to high school dropout to teenage pregnancy (Achenbach 1991; Foster and Hagan 2007; Hagan and Wheaton 1993; McLeod and Kaiser 2004; Nagin and Tremblay 2001; South 2002). Thus, childhood behavioral problems—even at early ages—paint a portrait of the problems children face both now and in the distant future.

Behavioral problems are important in part because of how common they are. As we mentioned, nearly all parents can remember a time when their children had one kind of behavioral problem or another. Yet, because the children of incarcerated parents are likely to have faced a number of troubles even if their parents had never been incarcerated, it is also be useful to know how parental incarceration affects the risk of experiencing events that are much less common but much more serious. In chapters 5 and 6, we considered the consequences of parental incarceration for infant mortality and child homelessness, events that are rare, tragic, almost always avoidable, and highly unequally distributed by race (Heron et al. 2009; Schempf et al. 2007; Wise 2003). In so doing, we provided insight into the effects of parental incarceration on not just risks that are common to all children but also risks that are far more likely among the most marginalized children and disrupt their lives significantly more.

As with chapter 3, the results from chapters 4, 5, and 6 were sobering and suggested that the incarceration of parents has profound consequences for their children. Across a variety of stringent models, having a father incarcerated was associated with substantial increases in children's behavioral problems. What's more, these effects were global: we linked paternal incarceration with sometimes dramatic increases in children's externalizing, internalizing, physically aggressive, and total behavioral problems. These effects are especially relevant because many children of incarcerated parents already had behavioral problems: the uptick in these problem behaviors caused by parental incarceration may elevate the behaviors to clinically relevant levels in these children—and lead to their being labeled "problem children" at very young ages. The one caveat is that we also saw signs that the incarceration of a father did significantly less damage—to the point of being a wash—when he had engaged in domestic violence. This suggests, as did the qualitative data in chapter 3, that the consequences of paternal incarceration in the presence of abuse are more complex than they are in its absence.

The same is the case for infant mortality. Across a range of statistical modeling strategies, paternal incarceration was associated with a significant and substantial increase in the risk of infant mortality. The magnitude of this effect varies somewhat across models, but the basic fact remains that infants of recently incarcerated parents are far more likely to die before their first birthday than are otherwise comparable children who did not have a parent incarcerated, even after adjusting for a host of observable characteristics of parents and children. According to our estimates, the effects of paternal incarceration on children's risk of infant mortality are comparable to the effects of maternal smoking on this risk. That these effects line up with such an important risk factor for infant mortality speaks volumes about their magnitude. As with behavioral and mental health problems, however, domestic violence moderates this relationship. When the father had never engaged in domestic violence, the effects of parental incarceration on infant mortality were large; when he had engaged in domestic violence at some point, it isn't clear whether his incarceration increases of decreases his child's risk of infant mortality.

Effects of paternal incarceration on child homelessness diverge somewhat from effects on behavioral problems and infant mortality. The average effect of paternal incarceration on children's risk of being homeless was substantial, as it was for the previous outcomes. Yet these effects were *not* moderated by domestic violence, and were concentrated among African American children. The lack of a moderating effect of domestic violence is somewhat perplexing, but the concentration of the effects among African

American children is more noteworthy for our findings because of its possible implications for inequality.

Of course, parental imprisonment could be unequally distributed, do significant damage to children, and still have relatively small consequences for racial inequality among children. Indeed, this is exactly what previous research on the consequences of mass imprisonment for black-white inequality among adult men has found (Wildeman and Muller 2012). Black men are much more likely to ever go to prison than white men are (Pettit and Western 2004; Western and Wildeman 2009). And going to prison does significant harm to men's subsequent life chances in a variety of domains. Aside from the well-documented consequences of prior incarceration for subsequent labor market outcomes (Pager 2003; Western 2006), incarceration is now linked with being in worse health (Massoglia 2008) and being less civically engaged (Manza and Uggen 2006). Yet despite the combination of concentrated imprisonment among black men and negative effects of having ever been imprisoned for men's subsequent life-chances, the effects of imprisonment on inequality among adult men are small. At least for lifetime earnings inequality, estimates put black-white inequality at 3 percent larger as a result of mass imprisonment (Western 2006), with effects of marital formation comparably small (Lopoo and Western 2005).

Results from chapter 7 paint a bleaker picture of the effects of mass imprisonment on the future of inequality in America. Indeed, they suggest that the long-term consequences of mass imprisonment for inequality may be even greater than the contemporaneous effects. For black-white inequalities in children's behavioral problems, we find that mass imprisonment increased inequalities in total behavioral problems by between 5 and 10 percent. These effects, of course, do not dwarf the consequences of imprisonment for inequality among adult men. (They are larger, to be sure, but they are still in the same ballpark.) The same could hardly be said for externalizing and internalizing behavioral problems, however. Based on our estimates, black-white disparities in children's internalizing behavioral problems would be between 14 percent and 26 percent smaller absent mass imprisonment. And black-white gaps in externalizing behavioral problems would be a shocking 24 percent to 46 percent smaller absent mass imprisonment. Thus, at least for children's behavioral problems, the consequences of mass imprisonment for racial disparities among children are likely to be substantially larger for children than they are for adult men.

The same applies, albeit to a somewhat lesser degree, for racial disparities in infant mortality rates and, to a greater degree, for child homelessness. According to estimates garnered using macro-level data, the black-white gap in the infant mortality rate would be between 9 percent and 18 percent smaller had the prison boom not taken place. According to estimates garnered using micro-level data, this gap would be between 7 percent and 13 percent lower had mass imprisonment not taken place. Effects on the black-gap in the risk of child homelessness are much larger, although these more modest effects on infant mortality are not insubstantial. According to our estimates, the black-white gap in child homelessness would have been between 26 percent and 65 percent smaller had mass imprisonment not taken place, a substantial and sobering shift in those inequalities.

Given the tremendous amount of money spent trying to shrink the black-white gaps in child homelessness and infant mortality and the importance of children's behavioral problems for their well-being in adolescence and adulthood, it would be fair to call these effects substantial. Indeed, they are so large that it may be reasonable to conclude that parental imprisonment is a distinctively American force for promoting intergenerational social inequality in the same league with decaying urban public school systems and highly concentrated disadvantage in urban centers as factors that distinctively touch—and disadvantage—poor black children.

More troubling is that the (conservative) point estimates provided here for effects on mental health and behavioral problems, infant mortality, and homelessness almost certainly underestimate the mass incarceration influence on the intergenerational transmission of social inequality for two reasons. First, for the outcomes we highlight in the book, mental health and behavioral problems, infant mortality, and homelessness, we have done everything possible to provide the most conservative estimate possible and generally focused on direct effects, even though the indirect effect of paternal incarceration for children is likely to be substantial. In light of this, it is reasonable to expect that the effects we discuss for these outcomes are likely to be smaller than the true effects. Second, and more importantly, the effects of paternal incarceration are almost certainly not limited to the outcomes presented here. As we described in the introduction, we limited our analysis to (1) the most proximate causes of problems for child well-being and (2) those that we could show the causal influence of paternal imprisonment on children with reasonable certainty. Yet ample evidence links the problems we describe to poor outcomes in adulthood *and* to other studies showing that parental imprisonment in childhood leads to poor educational attainment (e.g., Foster and Hagan 2007) or criminal involvement (e.g., Murray and Farrington 2008) in adulthood. If these effects are causal, then the influence of mass imprisonment on social inequality is much larger than even the disturbing estimates that we provide here would suggest.

UNDOING THE DAMAGE

Mass imprisonment has exacerbated inequality among adult men in America. And our results suggest that it has even more important implications for the future of inequality: the children of the prison boom are likely to be at elevated risk throughout their adolescence and adulthood—in no small part because of the incarceration of a parent. Yet, despite this dreary picture, we think that there are some social and criminal justice policies that could fairly easily be implemented to diminish the long-term consequences of mass imprisonment for American inequality. First, we focus on policies that would help all vulnerable children, not just those who have a parent in prison. Second, we discuss shifts in policing and correctional policy that would go far in preventing the outcomes we describe and result in significant cost savings in an era of strained budgets. Finally, in outlining the path forward, we start with the broadest possible programs, which are meant to address the causes of crime—since without crime, there can be little incarceration— by improving the most disadvantaged neighborhoods. We simultaneously suggest broader social welfare policy shifts and narrow criminal justice shifts. Most importantly, though imprisonment is the cause of the problems we detail here, solutions are not found in the criminal justice system.

The easiest policies to prescribe are those meant to enhance well-being for all disadvantaged children, not just those with a parent in prison. Broader community investment in the form of substantial increases in spending on educational, social welfare, drug treatment, and work-training programs would reduce harm among all children, not just the children of the prison boom. A call for greater public investment in children is particularly timely, as the same political culture that led to the prison boom also produced an unrelenting trend toward public disinvestment in children. In a review of research on children and families, David Demo and Martha Cox, citing the work of historian Stephanie Coontz, noted that "since the mid-1970s, politicians, employers, and nonparents have grown increasingly indifferent towards the needs of the next generation" (Demo and Cox 2000: 877; Coontz 1997). The same processes that produced a generation of children with a parent in prison did so at a time when social supports for vulnerable families were at their lowest levels in decades, doubly harming this newly vulnerable generation.

Calls to reinvest in public supports for children are not new but lack significant public support. Public opinion polls consistently show that Americans prioritize child welfare, broadly defined, but support tends to decline when helping poor children is viewed as helping poor adults (Heclo 1997). Public tolerance of some of the highest rates of child poverty among developed nations shows no sign of waning, for example (Rank 2005; Rank and Hirschl 1999; UNICEF 2012). We suspect the children of the incarcerated may suffer from the same problem—policies that help the children of the prison boom may be undermined to the extent that they can be reframed as helping "criminals." Part of the solution may be framing these programs not as charitable handouts but as smart public investment—thankfully, there is a good research base for this justification for programs aimed at improving cognitive and social-emotional development among vulnerable children. The best programs intervene early in the lives of disadvantaged children—with the provision of a high-quality preschool experience or home health visits for impoverished newborns—but have long-lasting benefits (e.g., Heckman 2006; Schweinhart et al. 2005). Interventions like these would support the children of the prison boom and reduce their mental health and behavioral problems, infant mortality, homelessness, and any number of other deleterious outcomes. More importantly, however, these recommendations would benefit all vulnerable children, not just those with an incarcerated parent.

Broad-based social interventions that improve cognitive or social-emotional outcomes for disadvantaged children may also diminish the rates of addiction, crime, and idleness that plague many urban, and increasingly, suburban and rural, communities. A second set of policy recommendations born out of our research is more directly focused on the criminal justice system. Diminishing incarceration through crime-reduction strategies as well as diverting more offenders away from the criminal justice system would directly improve the lives of many vulnerable children. As we have shown, the average incarcerated parent is not violent or abusive—their incarceration therefore has a negative effect on children and increases social inequality. Redirecting crime-control efforts and punishment toward the most violent of offenders may be the single most useful strategy for improving well-being and reducing inequality—it would remove parents who are destructive to their children from the home (as we showed in both chapter 4 and chapter 6) but allow many of the rest to remain.

Just as the educational and health-policy literature details promising results for increasing social and educational supports for disadvantaged children early in life, advances in policing mean that concrete strategies to reduce crime without increasing incarceration rates are possible. To take but one example, New York City is a source of fascination for today's criminologists because it has reduced crime by more than two-thirds while at the same time shrinking its prison population to well below the national average (Tierney 2013; Zimring 2012). Research on the crime drop in New York and elsewhere is ongoing, but mounting evidence points to advances in policing (including targeted or hot-spot policing, gun buy-back programs, and increasing the number of police on the streets) as a central factor (Zimring 2012; Braga 2012; Weisburd, Groff, and Yang 2012). Other analyses suggest that greater investment in policing as opposed to punishment is an effective strategy for reducing crime *and is also cheaper* to implement (Cook and Ludwig 2012). Quite contrary to the "nothing works" (Martinson 1974) mantra that characterized the dawn of the prison boom, today we know a lot more about what works for crime prevention and that many things in fact do—it is equally clear that the indiscriminate and lengthy imprisonment of millions of idle young men is no longer at the top of the list of effective criminal justice policies (Johnson and Raphael 2012; Sherman et al. 1998). The continuation of mass imprisonment simply makes no sense in the absence of large crime reduction effects and especially when coupled with the social problems created by mass incarceration detailed here.

Beyond supporting police work to prevent crime, we think the most important policies are those that seek to divert first-time offenders from incarceration. Two especially promising possibilities are providing the high-quality drug treatment programs that the residents of poor urban communities have long called for and implementing programs like Project HOPE, which offer swift, short, and certain sentences for probation violations. Drug and alcohol addiction is damaging not just to the individuals who suffer from addiction but also to their friends, families, and communities. High-quality drug programs, though no silver bullet, offer individuals the chance to clean themselves up without exposing them to the penal system. In short, treating addiction—and the increases in crime that often accompany it—as a public health problem instead of a criminal justice problem has the potential to diminish the long-term consequences of imprisonment because it could provide children with a parent who is neither addicted to drugs nor has a record. Of course, even the highest-quality treatment does not always work. And in the instances in which sobriety does not stick, we suggest that programs like Project HOPE be implemented. These programs offer swift, certain, and short jail stints for individuals who violate the conditions of their probation (Hawken and Kleinman 2009) and appear to deter crime much more effectively than most other programs. They offer a possible second step for those who continue to come into contact with the criminal justice system because of addiction.

Improved treatment options and Project HOPE offer an important way forward because they do not look the other way in the face of criminal activity but do not use incarceration as a first line of defense. This step is especially important in light of some of our findings. In our results and in other research on this topic two important trends emerge (Wildeman 2010). First, virtually all the negative effects of paternal incarceration on child well-being were concentrated among those incarcerated for nonviolent crimes. Second, the effects were also heavily concentrated among children whose fathers had not engaged in domestic violence in the household. To the degree that improved treatment for addiction and programs like Project HOPE shift the composition of the penal population away from those who commit nonviolent crimes of addiction and are not a danger to their families, the long-term consequences of mass imprisonment could be minimized. Other fairly simple changes, such as restricting parole revocation to the commission of new offenses, also offer an important step away from using incarceration as a first line of defense against crime, although we prefer policies that keep people from ever walking into a cell over the well-documented policies that may improve the quality of parent-child interaction once individuals have already been incarcerated (Comfort 2007, 2008; Nurse 2002).

Better treatment and more diversion from prison would go a long way toward reducing harms for children. Yet no discussion of mass imprisonment is complete without recognizing the large influence of sentencing policy, guidelines, and laws that have contributed to the prison boom. Our recommendations also include a return to the greater sentencing flexibility that characterized punishment before the boom. Sentencing policy during the prison boom relies on rigid guidelines and mandatory minimum prison terms for petty drug offenders. These policies offered little freedom to depart from prescriptions, drove more petty offenders to prison, and swept up a generation of black men. While sentencing flexibility runs the risk of social characteristics (such as race or education) driving sentence length, determinant sentences amplified punishment across the board while doing only little to reduce racial disparities in the prison population.

A public with a taste for ever-tougher sentences characterizes many descriptions of the cultural underpinnings of the prison boom, but the tide is turning. In 2012, voters in California voted to reform its Three Strikes law, formerly the toughest of its kind in the nation, so that only serious or violent crimes result in a lifelong prison sentence. In recognition of large racial disparities in prison terms for drug selling, Congress recently reduced sentencing disparities for crack versus cocaine use. Finally, in a poll released in late 2010, the Pew Center on the States found that the majority of voters now believe that public safety will not be compromised in any significant way if prison populations are greatly reduced. After years of intractability, reforming sentencing policy appears possible. Reforms are likely to reduce the cost of mass incarceration in state budgets; they may also be a boon for the next generation of vulnerable children by reducing the likelihood they will lose a parent to prison in the first place.

Programs such as Project HOPE, sentencing reform, and greater public willingness to embrace alternatives to prison offer a number of promising routes to reducing the costs of imprisonment to American inequality. Yet, as we have noted elsewhere, the great mistake of the prison boom was trying to solve deep-seated social problems with criminal justice policies (Wildeman and Western 2010). This is a mistake that those of us who seek to undo the consequences of mass imprisonment must avoid when we make policy recommendations. The prison is not the place to solve problems that have very little to do with crime—we do not therefore suggest that putting parenting programs in prison is the way to improve the lives of children of incarcerated parents. Too many mentally ill Americans already receive treatment only from a prison cell. The most common place for treatment for serious drug and alcohol addition should not be behind the walls of a prison. Prisons are as ill equipped to facilitate quality family functioning as they are at tackling serious mental illness or drug addiction.

Just as the prison boom was driven by sweeping social change as well as by shifts in sentencing policy, the solutions to mass incarceration must take place outside the criminal justice system. As we have shown, mass imprisonment has likely done great damage to American society. Indeed, the long-term consequences of this sea change in the use of imprisonment for social inequality appear so great that even its larger-than-estimated benefits for crime reduction would almost certainly not cover its social costs. The key to undoing these effects resides not in concentrating all our attention on criminal justice policies that focus only on those who do wrong but ignore those connected to them. Rather, investing heavily in the poor urban, suburban, and rural communities that have been left behind for so long will do much to undo the problems we have described here (and likely cost less while reducing future crime in the process). Indeed, without substantial public investments in these communities, it is unlikely that the long-term consequences of mass imprisonment will be undone, and the crushing poverty and lack of opportunities of today will be transformed into another generation of children of the prison boom.

METHODOLOGICAL APPENDIX

In this appendix, we include more detailed information on the data sources and models used to produce the estimates in chapters 2 through 7. We do not, however, display the results from full models when they are available elsewhere—generally in the form of journal articles—in the interest of keeping this methodological appendix as succinct as possible.

CHAPTER 2. THE SOCIAL PATTERNING OF PARENTAL IMPRISONMENT

Calculating the Risk of Parental Imprisonment

Chapter 2 relied on life-table methods to calculate the cumulative probability of experiencing paternal and maternal imprisonment by age fourteen for black and white American children born in 1978 and 1990. Life-table methods have long been used to study demographic processes such as fertility and mortality; they also can be used to study other aspects of life (Grieger and Danzinger

Table A1

DATA SETS USED TO CONSTRUCT ESTIMATES OF THE RISK OF PARENTAL IMPRISONMENT

Dataset	Used to Calculate
Surveys of Inmates in State and Federal Correctional Facilities (1979, 1986, 1991, 1997, 2004)	Proportion of prisoners imprisoned for the first time since child's birth in the last year
Sourcebook of Criminal Justice Statistics (2001)	Size of the year-end prison population
National Corrections Reporting Program (1983–2002)	Adjustment factor
Natality Detail File (1978, 1990)	Population at risk at birth
Life Tables of the United States (1978, 1990)	Child Mortality

2011; Pettit and Western 2004; Rank and Hirschl 1999; Manza and Uggen 2006; Bumpass and Lu 2000).

The key figure for estimating the cumulative risk of parental imprisonment is the number of children experiencing this event for the first time at any age. This quantity cannot be estimated using one data set, so we use the Surveys of Inmates in State and Federal Correctional Facilities (Bureau of Justice Statistics 1993, 1994, 1997, 2004a, 2007), the year-end counts of prisoners (Pastore and Maguire 2003; Maguire and Pastore 2001), and the National Corrections Reporting Program (Bureau of Justice Statistics 2004b). Table A1 lists the full list of data sources.

The most important data for constructing the numerator are drawn from the surveys of inmates. Since 1978, representative surveys of state inmates have been conducted—in 1979, 1986, 1991, 1997, and 2004; representative surveys of federal inmates were conducted in 1991, 1997, and 2004. State prisoners make up about

90 percent of the prison population; so including federal prisoners negligibly changes inmate characteristics. The population of children is calculated based on surveys of inmates, with an adjustment upward for the year-end inmate population. The surveys of inmates contain information about the prisoner's race and ethnicity, sex, education, prior prison admissions and releases, current prison admission, and number and ages of all children. We treat Hispanic blacks as black, which explains our slightly higher-end estimates for the number of incarcerated blacks. The 1979 and 1986 surveys collect information on up to six children; to maintain consistency, we stop counting children after six, so these numbers represent a slight undercount of the actual number of children experiencing the incarceration of a parent. Using these surveys, we estimate the proportion of prisoners in each survey experiencing imprisonment in the last year for the first time since the child was born. The number of children experiencing this event at any age is constructed by weighting all cases and then multiplying the weighted percentage by the number of individuals surveyed. Once this has been estimated, the number of children experiencing it can be estimated by race and education.

Each survey provides information about only one age, however.[1] Since each survey only provides an estimate for one age, we interpolate between survey years to estimate the number of children experiencing parental imprisonment at each age between birth and age fourteen.[2] The number of children born in 1978 experiencing parental imprisonment is based on the 1979, 1986, and 1991 surveys; for children born in 1990, the number is based on the 1991, 1997, and 2004 surveys. In light of possible error introduced by interpolation, it is worth nothing here that synthetic cohort estimates, which do not require interpolation, were very similar for all years.

Inmate surveys form the backbone of our estimate, but they have deficiencies. Since they are conducted early in the year, they underestimate the number of children experiencing parental imprisonment by the end of the year. To correct for this, we multiply our estimate by the year-end prison population divided by the number of prisoners participating in the surveys of inmates. Adjusting for prison growth makes the estimate more precise, but since surveys of inmates are conducted at one point in time, they underestimate short prison stays. To accurately estimate how many children experienced parental imprisonment for the first time, we must also include short stays. The National Corrections Reporting Program provides information on all prison admissions and releases from 1983 to 2002. Using these data, we are able to estimate the proportion of first-time prison admissions released in less than one year. Once we have this proportion, we can calculate the adjustment factor. The adjustment factor is the number of prison admissions divided by the number of admissions minus the number of prisoners who are released in less than one year. Our adjustment factor replicates the adjustment factor shown elsewhere (Bonczar 2003; Pettit and Western 2004). Unfortunately, we cannot estimate an adjustment factor before 1983 and after 2002, so we use the 1983 adjustment factor for years before 1983 and the 2002 adjustment factor for years after 2002. The largest and smallest adjustment factors differ by only 10 percent, so this extrapolation introduces minimal error.

Inmate surveys yield estimates of the number of children having a parent sent to prison by age fourteen; but they alone cannot estimate the cumulative percentage of children having a parent imprisoned. To calculate this percentage, we also need information about birth cohorts. Data from the National Vital Statistic's Natality Detail File provides this information (US Department of Health and Human Services 2002). We also need to know how many of these children survived to each age. Data from the 1978 and 1990 American life tables provide information about child mortality (U.S. Department of Health and Human Services 1982, 1994). Knowing how many children survived to each age, we are then able to estimate the number of children at risk of parental imprisonment at a given age by subtracting the number of children having experienced parental imprisonment from the number of children surviving to that age.

Our analysis focuses on racial and educational inequality in the risk of paternal and maternal imprisonment. Children from the 1978 and 1990 birth cohorts are coded as black if either parent is black; as white if both parents are white. Coding children's race this way produces conservative estimates of inequality because it overestimates the size of white birth cohorts. Although most mothers reported their race, race is unknown for 11 percent of fathers in 1978 and 15 percent of fathers in 1990. When paternal race is not reported, we assume that the child is the same race as the mother. This assumption likely has little effect on the results.

More data are missing on paternal education. In 1978, paternal education was missing 24 percent of the time; in 1990, paternal education was missing 22 percent of the time. We deal with missing data on father's education in three ways. First, we assume that fathers who are missing on education are comparable to men of the same race who report education—that data are missing completely at random. This assumption likely overestimates paternal education, since mothers may be less likely to report low paternal education than high paternal education. Second, we assume that fathers who are missing on education have similar levels of education to the mothers of their children, which probably underestimates paternal education, since mean paternal education exceeds mean maternal education. A third method, used for estimates reported here, assumes that missing education is halfway between what the first and second assumptions predict. Although estimates differ somewhat depending on how missing data are dealt with, the basic findings remain unchanged. Nonetheless, the level of missing data on paternal education indicates that findings about class inequality should be interpreted cautiously since changes in class inequality may be more pronounced than these estimates suggest. Once we know the number of children experiencing parental imprisonment for the first time by age and the number of children at risk of experiencing it, constructing a life table is straightforward since we can construct age-specific risks of first-time parental imprisonment. For more detail on these estimates, interested readers may consult Wildeman (2009).

CHAPTER 3. BEFORE AND AFTER IMPRISONMENT

Qualitative Interview Recruitment and Analysis

In 2004 and 2005, the Council on Crime and Justice (Minneapolis, Minnesota) completed three sets of interviews with children of incarcerated parents and their primary caregivers (see Nesmith and Ruhland [2008] for additional analyses using these data). In partnership with the Council on Crime and Justice, the first author conducted a fourth follow-up interview with the children and their primary caregivers about their experiences with incarceration during the summer of 2006. The interviews focused on the impact of parental incarceration on child well-being, mental health, and problem behaviors of children and their caregivers. Additional questions examined the financial well-being of families and the school performance of children before and after experiencing parental incarceration. The first, second, and third interviews were administered and analyzed by the Council on Crime and Justice and consisted of three sets of guided interviews with thirty-four children with an incarcerated parent and twenty-one caregivers over a period of twelve months. The children were aged seven to seventeen when their parent(s) were incarcerated and ranged from ten to twenty years old. All the children had a father incarcerated, and two also had a mother in prison.

For the initial interview, subjects were recruited by the Council using convenience sampling methods. Advertisements describing the study and soliciting participants were delivered to a variety of community organizations (including the YMCA, the Boys and Girls Club, the Urban League, and Big Brothers/Big Sisters). Advertisements were also posted in grocery stores, family restaurants, laundries, and libraries throughout Minneapolis and Saint Paul, Minnesota. Flyers were concentrated in neighborhoods that were identified as having high concentrations of incarcerated men and women. The children were asked about the following:

- Living arrangements prior to parental incarceration
- Relationship with parent prior to incarceration (time spent together, relationship quality), changes since incarceration (time spent together, rules, finances, family conflict), type and frequency of contact with incarcerated parent
- Relationship with peers
- School experiences (changes since incarceration), parent involvement in school (homework, attendance, and encouragement)
- Emotional support (knowledge of others in similar situation, talking to others about parental incarceration, role models)

With support from the Council, the first author conducted follow-up interviews with the children and their primary caregivers about their experiences with incarceration. The fourth round of interviews again focused on well-being, mental health, and problem behaviors and also gathered more information about the child's school experiences, attainment, and perceived economic consequences of parental incarceration. Additionally, as there is little information on parent-child relationships within the context of imprisonment and postrelease, the interviews were loosely structured with the goal of identifying the key aspects of the relationship to guide future research and inform quantitative analysis on the topic. The goal of the interviews was to isolate the most important mechanisms through which parental incarceration affects children and to inform the quantitative analysis. The fourth round of interviews covered the following:

- *Emotional effects of imprisonment*: experiences of children and caregivers with anxiety/depression and general physical and mental health
- *Problem behaviors as a result of imprisonment*: changes in levels of aggression and/or delinquency in children, family conflict as a result of imprisonment, school problems related to aggression (such as fighting)
- *Conditioning factors (or moderators)*: factors that may condition the effect of parental incarceration on children, such as age of the child
- *Relationship quality and depth*: changes in the relationship between parent and child and parent and primary caregiver prior to, during, and after incarceration, as measured by contact, emotional support, and conflict
- *Barriers and difficulties to parent-child relationship maintenance*: child visitation and frequency of parent-child visits during the incarceration, as well as postrelease experiences, quality of the relationship between the incarcerated parent and the child's primary caregiver (in most cases, the child's mother)
- *Involvement of incarcerated parent*: level of knowledge the incarcerated parent possesses on the child's current well-being and day-to-day activities and changes in parental involvement before, during, and after incarceration
- *Household changes and socioeconomic impact*: impact of incarceration on the current living situation of children and the influence of household disruptions on the child's overall well-being, economic consequences of parental incarceration and inclusion of a qualitative measure of perceived socioeconomic status designed for children
- *Reintegration*: level of difficulty the primary caregiver anticipates/experienced in re-establishing a parent-child bond after imprisonment, level of support for family reintegration on the part of the child and primary caregiver

Table A2

DESCRIPTION OF FAMILIES INTERVIEWED IN ALL FOUR WAVES

Family Members: Relationship and Age of children in 2006	Relationship to Incarcerated Parent	Incarceration Length, Crime, and History	Residency at time of Incarceration
Maxwell Family: Martha (biological aunt and adoptive mother) Nathanial (age 14)	Nathaniel's father and Martha's brother	Incarcerated for assault with a weapon in August 1999, release date in 2013 but eligible for parole in 2008. Incarcerated multiple times previously.	Was not living with son
Johnson Family: Michelle (biological mother) Tanya (age 12) Eric (age 11)	Tanya and Eric's father	Incarcerated for drug selling in 2000. Sentenced for 144 months. Incarcerated for three years previously.	Not living together at time of second incarceration.
Harrison Family: Susan (biological mother) Michael (11) David (9)	Michael and David's father and Susan's husband.	Incarcerated for kidnapping and criminal sexual contact in March 1998. Released in February 2003, sent back to prison for parole violations, and released in 2005. Incarcerated once previously.	Living with mother and children

Continued

Table A2 *Continued*

Family Members: Relationship and Age of children in 2006	Relationship to Incarcerated Parent	Incarceration Length, Crime, and History	Residency at time of Incarceration
Howard Family: Nina (biological mother) Shaundra (12)	Nina's husband and Shaundra's step-father.	Incarcerated for drug selling with a firearm in October 2001. Sentenced to 82 months. Served 4 months in halfway house. Moved back home in March 2006. Short jail sentence previously.	Living with mother and children
Jacobson Family: Alana (biological mother), Alex (9), Andrew (9), and Isaac (6)	Alana's fiancée and father of all three boys.	Incarcerated for murder and attempted murder in September 1999. Eligible for parole in 2035. Short jail sentence previously.	Living with mother and children.
Freeman Family: Allison (biological mother), Kayla (17), and Kevin (19)	Allison's husband and Kayla and Kevin's father.	Incarcerated for criminal sexual contact with a minor in January 2002. Release expected in 2008. No previous incarceration.	Living with mother and children

Anderson Family:			
Melissa (biological mother), Jacob (15), and Luke (10)	Melissa's boyfriend and Jacob and Luke's father.	Incarcerated in 1996 for attempted murder and pimping. Sentenced to 25 to life in prison. Jailed multiple times previously.	Living with mother but not with children.
Smith Family:			
Barbara (biological grandmother of child and biological mother of incarcerated parent), Colin (12)	Barbara's son and Colin's father.	Incarcerated for drug selling in 2000. Released in 2006. Incarcerated multiple times previously.	Not living with son.

Of the original twenty-one families initially interviewed by the Council on Crime and Justice in 2004 and 2005, seventeen (81%) completed a second interview, and fifteen (71%) completed a third interview. Primary caregiver participants in the Council's interviews were compensated $20 for the first interview, $30 for the second interview, and $60 for the final interview. Child participants were given $20 Target gift cards for the first and second interviews, and a $40 Target gift card for the final interview. Because the Council did not wish to deny any children who wanted to participate entry into the study, all children willing to be interviewed from each family were eligible for the study, provided that they were above the age of seven. This strategy resulted in the exclusion of no children because of age. Table A2 describes these families.

During summer 2006, an intern from the Council on Crime and Justice attempted to contact and recruit all of the original twenty-one families for participation in a final follow-up interview. Of the twenty-one families, eight agreed to be interviewed, six were located but did not respond to numerous attempts to recruit them into the study (we considered these cases "passive refusals"), and the remaining seven could not be located. Of the six that were located but did not respond, it is unclear in four cases whether it was the correct family. Participants in the original study provided contact information for themselves as well as for a family member or friend who would know how to locate them in the future. Despite this, the majority of families were difficult to locate two years after the original study. We suspect this is related to the socioeconomic disadvantage and residential instability of the population. For example, seven families did not have a working phone and did not respond to contact letters from the Council. In all other cases, both the families in the study as well as the contact family member or friend had moved leaving no forwarding address or did not have a working phone. Additional attempts were made to locate the families using the Internet and public records, but these were unsuccessful.

In all, eight primary caregivers and fourteen children completed a fourth interview. In one case, the father had recently been released from prison, and he also completed an interview. For the final round of interviews, caregivers (and the recently released father) were compensated $20 for participation, and children were offered a $10 Target gift card. One child was interviewed in a correctional facility and $10 was deposited in his facility account. Caregivers and children were interviewed simultaneously in separate rooms by the first author and a male intern from the Council on Crime and Justice. Participants were offered total freedom as to where the interview took place; seven chose to be interviewed in their homes and one family chose to be interviewed at the Council on Crime and Justice. As with prior interviews, we interviewed every child who was willing to participate. Primary caregivers and children were advised that they could choose not to answer any question, could stop the interview at any time, and that all interviews were tape-recorded. In the analysis for this chapter, we focus on the eight families who completed all four interviews, but the first author drew from interviews with the entire sample to develop the conclusions herein.

CHAPTER 4. EFFECTS ON MENTAL HEALTH AND BEHAVIORAL PROBLEMS

Description of Measures, Methods, and Robustness Tests

Independent Variables. The PHDCN and the FFCW do not provide information on the length of the prison sentence or a detailed criminal history. The analyses therefore estimate the average effects of paternal incarceration on children and include men who served a few days in jail as well as those with lengthy prison sentences. Despite these weaknesses, the PHDCN and the FFCW represent the best available survey data to study the effects of paternal incarceration on children for several reasons. First, the incarceration of a father can be fixed at a particular point in time, limiting the extent to which preexisting disadvantages are conflated with the effects of paternal incarceration. Second, the sampling frames, although different across data sources, ensure a large and diverse sample of children of incarcerated fathers and similarly situated peers for comparison. Third, these sources taken together provide estimates of the average effect of paternal incarceration on children across a range of ages from young children to adolescents. Finally, and most critically, the estimates of paternal incarceration effects are markedly similar across the data sources, even though the sampling frames, control variables, and ages differ.

The results in this chapter are drawn from Wildeman (2010) and Wakefield and Wildeman (2011). Interested readers may consult these publications for a full description of the variables included in each model, specific coefficients, and several robustness tests.

CHAPTER 5. PATERNAL INCARCERATION AND INFANT MORTALITY

Additional Information on the PRAMS Survey

First contact for the PRAMS survey is made with a letter introducing the project. An initial survey and "tickler" follow shortly thereafter. Those who do not return the first survey within seven to fourteen days are sent a second survey. If they fail to complete this survey, most states send a third one seven to fourteen days later.[3] All mothers who do not respond to the final mail survey are called seven to fourteen days later. The PRAMS survey tends to have response rates in the 70 percent to 80 percent range—well within the acceptable range—but it also has lower response rates for individuals from marginalized groups, as is often the case with surveys (Gilbert et al. 1999).

In considering the parental incarceration–infant mortality relationship, all models adjust for time at risk of mortality by controlling for the time between the birth and the mother's survey response. Since the risk of infant mortality diminishes nonlinearly over time (Wise 2003), all models include a squared term for exposure.[4] Given the inequalities in infant mortality rates across states and over time (Mathews and MacDorman 2007), we include state and year dummies.

In addition to controlling for exposure, state, and year, most models control for factors that precede the pregnancy and influence infant-mortality risk. Consistent with the body of research documenting the positive association between parental marital status and child outcomes (Cherlin 1999), research on infant mortality tends to find that infants of married parents are more likely to survive than those with unmarried parents (Frisbie 2005), so we adjust for marital status in most models. Research also finds that black infants are less likely to survive than white infants (Singh and Kogan 2007) and that Hispanic infants are more likely than white infants to survive if their mother was an immigrant (Hummer et al. 2007). Since the PRAMS data do not include information about nativity, we are unable to differentiate native-born and immigrant Hispanic mothers. We therefore adjust for maternal race/ethnicity: black, Hispanic, other, and white (reference). Research shows elevated risks of infant mortality for infants born to teen mothers and mothers over age forty (Hoyert et al. 2006), so initial models included dummies for these age groups. But since a model with linear and squared age terms better fit the data, captured elevated infant mortality risks for infants of very young and old mothers, and did not alter the parental incarceration–infant mortality relationship, we opted to include the linear and quadratic terms.

Unfortunately, the PRAMS data do not include a measure of household income, which associates with parental incarceration and infant mortality. In addition to limiting the sample to mothers who dropped out of high school, which diminishes heterogeneity in income, we dealt with this limitation by adjusting for maternal WIC (Women, Infants, and Children) receipt, which is both a proxy for poverty and associated with better birth outcomes and lower risks of infant mortality for mothers who are poor (Moss and Carver 1998). The final prepregnancy controls included represent a combination of birth order and prior poor birth outcomes. Specifically, we adjust for whether it is the mother's first birth, whether it is not the mother's first birth but she previously had a low-birth-weight or preterm infant, and whether it is not the mother's first birth and she has not had a low-birth-weight or preterm infant. Given the relationship between parity, prior poor birth outcomes, and infant mortality (Frisbie 2005), and the lack of information about the number of prior births in PRAMS, this strategy is appropriate. Results in which we instead controlled for any prior live births, preterm births, and low-birth-weight births did not alter the relationships of interest.

In addition to these background characteristics, some models adjust for relevant covariates that have to do with the current birth and have been consistently shown to be associated with the risk of infant mortality. We adjust for maternal weight gain because of its positive association with birth weight (Chomitz et al. 1995). We also include a squared term for maternal weight gain since doing so improved model fit, likely because very high and low weight gains are indicative of other factors placing infants at elevated mortality risk. Following the fundamental causes framework (Link and Phelan 1995, 2002; see also Frisbie et al. 2004) we also adjust for stressful life events that are likely to influence the risk of infant mortality: the mother's partner losing his job, the mother being homeless, and the mother or her partner having a drug or alcohol problem. We add these risk factors and include a squared term. In addition, we adjust for maternal smoking since prior research has found a strong association between maternal smoking and adverse birth outcomes (Chomitz et al. 1995; Kramer et al. 2000). We also adjust for whether the pregnancy was unintended, although research suggests a weak association between unintended pregnancy and birth outcomes (Frisbie 2005). Some models adjust for the adequacy of prenatal care because of the association between the adequacy of prenatal care and infant mortality (Alexander and Korenbrot 1995; Mathews and MacDorman 2007). We code prenatal care as "inadequate (reference)," "intermediate," "adequate," and "adequate plus" (Kotelchuck 1994).

Some models also adjust for whether the birth was paid for by Medicaid because of the elevated risk of adverse birth outcomes for women on Medicaid (Moss and Carver 1998). Ideally, we would also have adjusted for whether the birth was covered by private insurance in order to provide a more nuanced comparison (Frisbie et al. 1997), but such measures were not available for all survey years. The data are also limited in their measures of maternal morbidity and labor complications, both of which are strongly associated with the risk of infant mortality (Frisbie et al. 2004); so we adjust for whether the mother was hospitalized at any time during the pregnancy and whether the mother stayed in the hospital for more than three days for the birth. Although emphasizing the effect of birth weight on infant mortality to the neglect of other factors would be a mistake (Wise 2003), the fact remains that low (<3500 grams) and very low (<1500 grams) birth weight infants are at elevated mortality risk, as are preterm infants. In fact, despite the heavy emphasis on the effect of birth weight on mortality, some have claimed that preterm birth may be an even more important factor shaping infant mortality (Callaghan et al. 2006). Regardless of which of these factors most strongly shapes infant mortality risks, we adjust for birth weight and preterm birth. Final models include a dummy variable for whether the mother reported that the father had engaged in domestic violence toward her because we expect that effects of parental incarceration on infant mortality are concentrated among children whose fathers did not engage in violence. Even though domestic violence is likely underreported here (as elsewhere), the reported rates of domestic violence are nonetheless high, with 15 percent of the sample reporting that they had been abused by the father of the child at some point (figure 5.4). Since PRAMS did not include questions about domestic violence in the core interviews until the 1995 survey, the sample upon which this stage is based is smaller ($N = 42,544$). We limit the sample to singleton births and children with no birth defects since the predictors of infant mortality may differ for these infants. And we use weights for all analyses using the PRAMS data to account for the complex sample design. For descriptive statistics for all dependent and independent variables used in the individual-level analyses and full model results, see Wildeman (2012).

CHAPTER 6. PARENTAL IMPRISONMENT AND CHILD HOMELESSNESS

Coding

For our analysis, we considered children to have been homeless if they fit the following criteria at sixty months: (1) one parent either reported living in temporary housing, a group shelter, or on the street at the time of the interview or reported having stayed somewhere not intended for regular housing—such as an abandoned building or car—for at least one night in the last twelve months; and (2) the same parent reported having lived with the child all or most of the time. Coding for this variable has been used in prior analyses (Fertig and Reingold 2008), but it has three limitations. First, it provides no insight into the duration of homelessness. Second, it underestimates cases of child homelessness in the last year because it counts staying in a shelter as being homeless only if the child was living in a shelter at the time of the interview. Although this underestimate is unlikely to substantially bias our results (and to bias them down), it bears mentioning because it elucidates why the risks of child homelessness shown here for a vulnerable group of children are only slightly higher than they are for the population of children in two cities (Culhane and Metraux 1999: 228, 230). Finally, the measure cannot guarantee that the child was living with the parent when the parent was homeless. Additional analyses suggest that although the child may not have been living with the parent while they were homeless, it is an excellent measure of *family* homelessness since in more than three-quarters of the families in which the child was considered homeless, he or she were living with his or her mother at the time of the interview.

Fathers and mothers were considered to have ever been incarcerated by thirty months if they or the other parent reported that they had ever been incarcerated at the baseline, twelve-month, or thirty-month interviews or were incarcerated at thirty months. Caretakers self-rated health were based on reports of whether their health was excellent to poor. If both parents claimed to live with the child all or most of the time, then the mean of their self-rated health scores was used. This method was used for the rest of the controls unless otherwise noted. Either parent was considered to have a drug or alcohol problem if either parent agreed that drugs or alcohol interfered with work, personal relationships, or made it difficult to manage life on a daily basis, or he or she had such a strong desire to drink that they had to have a drink. Mothers were considered to have been abused by the father if they reported having been hurt by the father in a fight since the child's birth. The household income-to-poverty ratio was constructed by dividing household income by the poverty line for a family of the same size. Difficulty paying bills was based on caretaker reports that they couldn't pay all of their rent or mortgage; couldn't pay all their gas, oil, or electricity bills; had their gas, oil, or electricity turned off for nonpayment; or had their telephone disconnected because of lack of payment. Lack of social support was based on whether caregivers thought they could count on someone to loan them $200, provide them with a place to live, provide emergency childcare, or cosign a loan for $1000 with them. Maternal life dissatisfaction was based on whether mothers responded that they were "very satisfied" to "very dissatisfied" overall with their lives.

Maternal stress was based on a reverse-coded scale of questions asking mothers whether being a parent was much harder than they thought it would be, they felt trapped by their responsibilities as a parent, taking care of their children was much more work than pleasure, and they often felt tired, worn out, or exhausted from raising a family.

Unfortunately, the best measures of paternal and maternal self-control, which may have a strong influence on the risk of experiencing incarceration (Gottfredson and Hirschi 1990), are not available until later survey waves.[5] This is unfortunate because it leaves it up for debate whether the analysis should adjust for self-control. On the one hand, criminological theories suggest that self-control is stable from childhood (Gottfredson and Hirschi 1990), even if social ties shape how it influences behavior (Sampson and Laub 1990). According to this perspective, including the controls for paternal and maternal self-control would be appropriate—even if they were measured *after* parental incarceration. On the other hand, research suggests not only that self-control is not as stable as it was once thought to be but also that it may change as a result of incarceration. And though some analyses show an increase in self-control during incarceration (Mitchell and MacKenzie 2006), the dominant opinion is that incarceration diminishes self-control, as individuals adjust to survive the brutalizing prison environment (e.g., Nurse 2002: 54–56). Since incarceration might inhibit self-control but also plays a strong role in influencing the risk of incarceration, we chose to exclude those controls from the main results presented in this chapter but to include them in a series of robustness checks, all of which can be found in Wildeman (forthcoming).

Methods

We use a series of logistic regression models to consider the effects of recent paternal and maternal incarceration on child homelessness. All models use clustered standard errors to account for the clustering of observations on cities. We also estimate models that restrict the sample to children of ever-incarcerated parents (who might differ from other parents in myriad ways), and, in so doing, we diminish unobserved heterogeneity, thereby substantially strengthening causal inference (LaLonde 1986; Leamer 1983). By restricting the sample to children who have not recently been homeless, we show that results are not driven by children with a history of unstable housing, who were, perhaps unsurprisingly, disproportionately children of incarcerated parents. Yet we also wanted to know just how large these effects are. Since the dependent variable is dichotomous, to get changes in the risk of child homelessness from the logistic regression models, we generate estimates of the probability of child homelessness for those experiencing and not experiencing paternal incarceration under two scenarios: holding all values at the sample mean and holding all values at the mean for those experiencing recent paternal incarceration.

CHAPTER 7. MASS IMPRISONMENT AND CHILDHOOD INEQUALITY

Further Information on the State-Level Analysis for Infant Mortality

We could only construct a measure of racial inequality in the infant mortality rate for between thirty-one and thirty-three states (depending on the year) because of the number of states that did not have enough black births and/or infant deaths for all years to provide a reliable measure of the black infant mortality rate, so the N for those analyses is smaller ($N = 446$). Although these states contain about 90 percent of the population of the United States in any year, the results for inequality in the infant mortality rate do not generalize to states with a small total population or a small black population. Unlike the individual-level analysis, where the controls that should be included were clear because of the extensive literature on infant mortality, the state-level portion of this analysis confronts a host of obstacles when selecting control variables. These include the dearth of research considering the factors shaping the infant mortality rate (Frisbie 2005); the often substantial differences in the predictive power of these factors, depending on the method utilized to consider that relationship (for an example, see the debate on the GINI and population health (Beckfield 2004; Wilkinson 1992, 2009); and the problem of introducing multicollinearity into models when attempting to adjust for all relevant control variables. In dealing with the first of these two issues, which are related in a certain degree, we opted to include controls that were either (1) likely associated with both the imprisonment rate and the infant mortality rate or (2) plausibly associated with the imprisonment rate and had been shown to be associated with the infant mortality rate in models that included place fixed effects. Using this criterion for the inclusion of controls made good sense given serious concerns about multicollinearity (see table A3) but it meant that the final models shown in this chapter do not include the vast number of highly correlated controls often included in the public health literature (for example, Bird 1995) or measures of the political factors that have been shown to shape welfare state spending, spending on prisons, and the imprisonment rate (Beckett 1997; Ellwood and Guetzkow 2009; Greenberg and West 2001; Guetzkow 2011; Soss, forthcoming; Wacquant 2009).

To deal with concerns about multicollinearity, we did two things. First, when possible, we constructed scales instead of including controls separately in an attempt to use the high correlations between variables to our advantage. Second, and to be discussed in detail later, we also utilized a first difference model since first difference models do not generally suffer from the same problems with multicollinearity as traditional models (tables A3 and A4). To return to the controls included, let us first start by outlining the controls that seemed sufficiently important to include separately in the model. These include the violent crime rate, GDP per capita (in 1000s of 2000 dollars), the unemployment rate, total

Table A3

CORRELATION MATRICES FOR VARIABLES UTILIZED IN STATE-LEVEL ANALYSES IN THE MAIN (A) AND FIRST DIFFERENCE (B) MODELS

Panel A

	Fem. Imp.	Male Imp.	Total Imp.	Crime	GDP	Unemp.	Health	AFDC	Poverty	Birth	Heterog.
Fem. Imp.	1.0000										
Male Imp.	0.8066	1.0000									
Total Imp.	0.8269	0.9994	1.0000								
Crime	0.3566	0.6707	0.6727	1.0000							
GDP	0.2909	0.6890	0.1826	0.6913	1.0000						
Unemp.	0.0603	0.1882	0.6463	0.4646	0.0863	1.0000					
Health	0.3212	0.6593	-0.2721	0.5392	0.8953	0.0898	1.0000				
AFDC	-0.3854	-0.2619	0.6217	0.0254	0.2305	0.0820	0.1632	1.0000			
Poverty	0.3494	0.6317	0.8529	0.7508	0.4016	0.5604	0.3283	-0.2842	1.0000		
Birth	0.6392	0.8565	0.1804	0.7270	0.5790	0.2928	0.5850	-0.3790	0.7785	1.0000	
Heterog.	0.0566	0.1861		0.3170	0.4249	0.1683	0.3330	0.5028	-0.0723	0.0159	1.0000

Continued

TABLE A3 Continued

Panel B

	Fem. Imp.	Male Imp.	Total Imp.	Crime	GDP	Unemp.	Health	AFDC	Poverty	Birth	Heterog.
Fem. Imp.	1.0000										
Male Imp.	0.6414	1.0000									
Total Imp.	0.6929	0.9976	1.0000								
Crime	0.0823	-0.0496	-0.0392	1.0000							
GDP	-0.0709	-0.0350	-0.0393	-0.1347	1.0000						
Unemp.	0.0088	-0.0858	-0.0798	0.2492	-0.4263	1.0000					
Health	0.1587	0.0262	0.0389	0.2738	-0.1982	0.4696	1.0000				
AFDC	0.0085	0.0156	0.0154	0.0322	-0.1295	0.2326	0.1531	1.0000			
Poverty	0.0338	-0.0706	-0.0634	0.2777	-0.3457	0.4288	0.3919	0.0879	1.0000		
Birth	0.1908	0.0928	0.1044	0.1381	-0.1635	0.1085	0.1370	0.0340	0.1518	1.0000	
Heterog.	-0.0329	-0.0169	-0.0189	-0.0711	0.0435	0.0279	-0.1964	-0.0452	0.1096	-0.0320	1.0000

health care expenditures per capita (in 1000s of 2000 dollars), and the combined TANF/AFDC monthly benefit for a family of four (in 100s of 2000 dollars). We control for the violent crime rate because of the high correlation between the violent crime rate and the imprisonment rate ($r = .66$) and the fact that the violent crime rate may be positively correlated with the infant mortality rate. Although the consensus is that the effects of GDP per capita are of greatest importance for population health in the early stages of economic development (Pampel and Pillai 1986), the dramatic state-level disparities in GDP per capita nonetheless suggested that it would be worthwhile adjusting for this factor, especially since it provides a context against which to discuss the measures of poverty (discussed more later). Likewise, we adjust for the unemployment rate since cyclical fluctuations may be important in shaping population health, although it remains unclear whether increases in the unemployment rate may actually benefit population health (Ruhm 2000) or harm it by increasing poverty. We also adjust for total public expenditures on health and the combined TANF/AFDC monthly benefit for a family of four. The connections between welfare-state spending (as measured by total state spending on health) and population health, though contentious, have consistently been found to be statistically significant in the most rigorous studies, with increases in total public expenditures on health shown to strongly decrease the infant mortality rate (Conley and Springer 2001). The connections between the generosity of the cash welfare system and the infant mortality rate is less well-established, but given the micro-level relationship between welfare receipt and infant mortality (Moss and Carver 1998) and the fact that increases in correctional expenditures may diminish spending on welfare because of an increasing imprisonment rate (Ellwood and Guetzkow 2009; Guetzkow 2011), we also control for the generosity of the state cash welfare system in all models presented here in order to keep our results conservative.

All state-level models also control for three indices: a poverty index, a high-risk birth index, and a heterogeneity index. Initial

Table A4

STANDARDIZED REGRESSION COEFFICIENTS FOR FEMALE, MALE, AND TOTAL IMPRISONMENT RATES BASED ON STATE-LEVEL MODELS SHOWN IN TABLES 4 AND 5 AND FIRST DIFFERENCE MODELS

	Table 4				Table 5			
	Model 1	Model 2	Model 3	Model 4	Model 1	Model 2	Model 3	Model 4
Main Results								
Female Imp. (t -1)	.08*	—	—	—	—	—	—	—
Male Imp. ($t-1$)	—	.16**	—	—	—	—	—	—
Total Imp. ($t-1$)	—	—	.15**	.14*	.25***	.39**	.03	.34*
Total Imp. ($t+2$)	—	—	—	.07#	—	—	—	—
First Diff. Results								
Female Imp. ($t-1$)	.09#	—	—	—	—	—	—	—
Male Imp. ($t-1$)	—	.36***	—	—	—	—	—	—
Total Imp. ($t-1$)	—	—	.35***	.35***	.41***	.57***	.79***	.33**
Total Imp. ($t+2$)	—	—	—	.04	—	—	—	—

Notes: All t-tests for imprisonment are two-sided. Standard errors omitted in order to conserve space. All models include the full set of controls shown in Tables 4 and 5. For the full set of the coefficients from the first difference models, please contact the author.

* $p < .05$; ** $p < .01$; *** $p < .001$

models included each component of these indices separately, but given the high correlation between them, constructing indices provided one way to diminish multicollinearity while simultaneously providing the most rigorous set of controls possible. The poverty index is a combination of the percent of the population that is at least twenty-five years old that did not complete high school, the percent of the population that is black, the GINI, the percent of the population that is poor, and the number of AFDC/ TANF cases per 1000 (α = .71). Although much research in this area suggests the importance of adjusting for the GINI because of its association with the infant mortality (Wilkinson 1992) and imprisonment (Wilkinson 2009) rates, there is reason to expect that the percent of the population that is black, poor, or poorly educated would also be significantly associated with both the imprisonment and infant mortality rates. The high-risk birth index combines the percent of births that were nonmarital, to women who received no prenatal care, preterm, and low birth weight (α = .68). Given the strong effects of many of these factors in shaping the risk of infant mortality (Frisbie 2005; Wise 2003), this index seems especially likely to explain variability in the infant mortality rate. Although the initial high-risk birth index also included the percent of mothers who smoked because of the dramatic effects of maternal smoking on infant mortality (Chomitz et al. 1995; Kramer et al. 2000), including this factor did not increase the α or influence the effects of this index on the infant mortality rate, so the final version of this scale excludes the percent of mothers who smoked. The final scale gauges population heterogeneity and includes measures of the percent of the population that is foreign-born, Hispanic, and resides in an urban area (α = .74). Given the high correlations between many of the explanatory and control variables, we replicated all analyses presented in this paper using a first difference method, which almost entirely resolves potential multicollineaity (see table A4) with substantively identical results for most outcomes. Interested readers may also consult Wildeman (2012) for more detail.

NOTES

Introduction

1. Nathaniel is a pseudonym, as this young man is one of the interviewees described in chapter 3.
2. Diana Marcum, "Recent College Grad Becomes Youngest Councilman in Stockton History," *Los Angeles Times* online, November 8, 2012, http://articles.latimes.com/2012/nov/08/local/la-me-tubbs-20121108.
3. And, indeed, there is a large literature in psychology that considers the resilience of children like Michael.
4. More information about the episode and online resources can be found at www.sesamestreet.org/parents/topicsandactivities/toolkits/incarceration.
5. The results for maternal incarceration are much more complicated and largely beyond the scope of this book. Put simply, the more rigorous the study, the more likely the results are null, as we discuss in more detail in chapter 4 (see e.g., Cho 2009; Wildeman and Turney forthcoming).
6. It is for this reason, for instance, that we do not use the excellent data from the Cambridge Study in Delinquency Development, which were collected in the United Kingdom and have been

widely used to estimate the effects of paternal imprisonment on children (e.g., Murray and Farrington 2005).

7. We exclude the Scandinavian countries for similar reasons, as imprisonment rates there are low enough that even in the face of negative effects of paternal incarceration on children (e.g., Wildeman et al., forthcoming), the consequences of the penal system for childhood inequality cannot be particularly large.

8. The growth in the incarceration rate, furthermore, has endured despite fluctuations in crime and the economy and shifts in policing and correctional policy. Indeed, rising incarceration rates are the one constant during the period. This renders conventional explanations for imprisonment rates, like crime rates or business cycles, difficult to defend. The evidence suggests that the growth in incarceration in the United States is best conceived as a sometimes deliberate policy choice rather than a natural or automatic response to increases in the crime rate or a weakening labor market (Beckett 1997; Simon 2007; Garland 2000).

Chapter 2

1. Author's calculations using U.S. Department of Health and Human Services. 2010. The AFCARS (Adoption and Foster Care Analysis and Reporting System): Preliminary FY 2009 Estimates. http://www.acf.hhs.gov/programs/cb/stats_research/afcars/tar/report17.pdf.

2. Author's calculations using U.S. Department of Health and Human Services. 2010. The AFCARS (Adoption and Foster Care Analysis and Reporting System): Preliminary FY 2009 Estimates. http://www.acf.hhs.gov/programs/cb/stats_research/afcars/tar/report17.pdf.

3. See the introduction for a detailed description.

4. Estimating this quantity requires bringing together a number of different data sets, using complex life-table methods, and making difficult decisions when the data are limited in one regard or another. For those interested in the details of our estimation strategy, refer to the methodological appendix.

Chapter 3

1. The qualitative data are described in more detail in the methodological appendix.
2. For an analysis of these and additional interviews, see Nesmith and Ruhland (2008).
3. Terence is not the biological father of Nina's children but has performed in this role since they were young.

Chapter 4

1. Several studies link maternal incarceration to childhood disadvantage, most notably in increases in foster care caseloads, where it may drive childhood inequality in a far more meaningful way (Swann and Sylvester 2006; Johnson and Waldfogel 2002; Kruttschnitt 2010). There is also very good evidence that the effects of maternal incarceration on children are highly contextualized and heterogeneous (see, e.g., Arditti 2012); but, since considering effects on inequality necessitates a consideration of average effects, we do not discuss these studies in detail.
2. More recent waves of data collection also ask about maternal incarceration and the timing of incarceration.
3. We are unable to differentiate between prison and jail incarceration. Although this is certainly a limitation of the current analysis, none of the data sets that allow us to link the incarceration of a parent with changes in children's behavioral or mental health problems—or family processes more broadly—differentiates between the two.
4. It is worth noting that results using the CSDD data (Murray and Farrington 2008, 2005) and the Add Health data (Roettger and Swisher 2011; Foster and Hagan 2007, 2009; Roettger and Boardman 2012) are generally similar.
5. We focus on physically aggressive behaviors using the FFCW, but the results presented here are also apparent for a broad range of behavioral problems among FFCW children at ages three and five (Geller et al. 2009).

6. We standardized physical aggression because physical aggression changes so much between age three and age five that standardizing physical aggression is preferred for considering within-child change at young ages such as these. We used the full population of children, including both boys and girls, to standardize the measures of physical aggression, which explains why the average standardized physical aggression measures exceeds 1 for boys.
7. See Massoglia (2008) for an application to incarceration.
8. For results for girls, see Wildeman (2010).
9. See Wildeman (2010) for greater detail on these models and the results.

Chapter 5

1. For a list of participating states, see Wildeman (2012).
2. We use the term "early infant mortality" throughout the analyses because it does not measure the entire first year.

Chapter 6

1. The character, Lily, was introduced in a 2011 prime time special produced by the Sesame Street Workshop to draw attention to food insecurity in the United States. Notably, the character also modeled stress and stigma resulting from food insecurity, a common problem for homeless children as well. http://artsbeat. blogs.nytimes.com/2011/10/03/sesame-street-special-on-hunger-introduces-new-muppet-character/

Chapter 7

1. Although the percent increase in the risk of infant mortality presented in this chapter is similar to the odds ratios presented in chapter 5, we would like to assure readers that we have not conflated changes in odds with changes in percentages. Because the risk of the infant mortality is low, the change in the odds is highly comparable to the change in the percentages, as is well

established in research on rare events, including infant mortality.
2. Greater detail on the analysis can be found in the methodological appendix. In assembling the data set for this analysis, annual state-level data were pooled over the period 1990–2003.
3. See Wildeman (2012) for the full models.

Appendix

1. The year 1991 is the sole exception to this rule, as it estimates the number experiencing parental imprisonment at age thirteen for children born in 1978 as well at the number experiencing it at age one for children born in 1990.
2. See Pettit and Western (2004) for an application of this technique to data on adults.
3. Not all states send out a third mailer now. Fewer sent out a third mailer at the beginning of the period considered.
4. We centered the measure of duration before constructing the squared term in order to avoid introducing multicollinearity between the linear and squared terms, a practice we follow whenever including quadratics.
5. These measures were based on how parents responded to questions about how often they or the other parent did things without considering the consequences, got into trouble because they didn't think before they acted, did things that may cause trouble with the law, lied or cheated, got into fights, and didn't feel guilty when they misbehaved.

REFERENCES

Achenbach, Thomas M. 1991. Manual for the Child Behavior Checklist/14-18 and 1991 Profile. Burlington: University of Vermont Department of Psychiatry.

Alexander, Greg R., and Carl C. Korenbrot. 1995. The Role of Prenatal Care in Preventing Low Birth Weight. *Future of Children* 5:103–120.

Amato, Paul R., and Alan Booth. 2009. The Legacy of Parents' Marital Discord: Consequences for Children's Marital Quality. *Journal of Personality and Social Psychology* 81 (4):627–638.

American Psychological Association. 1996. Violence and the Family: Report of the American Psychological Association Presidential Task Force on Violence and the Family. Washington, DC: American Psychological Association.

Apel, Robert, Arjan A. J. Blokland, Paul Nieubeerta, and Marieke van Schellen. 2010. The Impact of Imprisonment on Marriage and Divorce: A Risk Set Matching Approach. *Journal of Quantitative Criminology* 26:269–300.

Arditti, Joyce A. 2012. *Parental Incarceration and the Family: Psychological and Social Effects of Imprisonment on Children, Parents, and Caregivers*. New York: New York University Press.

Arum, Richard, and Gary LaFree. 2008. Educational Attainment, Teacher-Student Ratios, and the Risk of Adult Incarceration among U.S. Birth Cohorts since 1910. *Sociology of Education* 81 (4):397–421.

Bahr, Howard M., and Theodore Caplow. 1974. *Old Men Drunk and Sober*. New York: New York University Press.

Barker, Vanessa. 2009. *The Politics of Imprisonment: How the Democratic Process Shapes the Way America Punishes Offenders*. New York: Oxford University Press.

Bartholet, Elizabeth. 1999. *Nobody's Children: Abuse and Neglect, Foster Drift, and the Adoption Alternative*. Boston: Beacon Press.

———. 2000. Reply: Whose Children? A Response to Professor Guggenheim. *Harvard Law Review* 113 (8):1999–2008.

Beckett, Katherine. 1997. *Making Crime Pay: Law and Order in Contemporary American Politics*. New York: Oxford University Press.

Beckfield, Jason. 2004. Does Income Inequality Harm Health? New Cross-National Evidence. *Journal of Health and Social Behavior* 45:231–248.

Binswanger, Ingrid A., Marc F. Stern, Richard A. Deoy, Patrick J. Heagerty, Allen Cheadle, Joann G. Elmore, and Thomas D. Koepsell. 2007. Release from Prison: A High RIsk of Death for Former Inmates. *New England Journal of Medicine* 356:157–165.

Bird, Sheryl T., and Bauman, Karl E. 1995. The Relationship Between Structural and Health Service Variables and State-Level Infant Mortality in the United States. *American Journal of Public Health* 85:26–29.

Blumstein, Alfred, and Jacqueline Cohen. 1973. A Theory of the Stability of Punishment. *Journal of Criminal Law, Criminology, and Police Science* 63 (2):198–207.

Bonczar, Thomas P. 2003. *The Prevalence of Imprisonment in the U.S. Population, 1974–2001*. Washington, DC: US Department of Justice.

Bowlby, John. 1988. *A Secure Base: Parent-Child Attachment and Healthy Human Development*. New York: Basic Books.

Braga, Anthony. 2012. Getting Deterrence Right? Evaluating Evidence and Contemporary Crime Control Mechanisms. *Criminology and Public Policy* 11 (2):201–210.

Braman, Donald. 2004. *Doing Time on the Outside: Incarceration and Family Life in Urban America*. Ann Arbor: University of Michigan Press.

Breen, Richard, and Jan O. Jonsson. 2005. Inequality of Opportunity in Comparative Perspective: Recent Research on Educational Attainment and Social Mobility. *Annual Review of Sociology* 31 (August):223–243.

Buckner, John C. 2008. Understanding the Impact of Homelessness on Children. *American Behavioral Scientist* 51:721–736.

Bumpass, Larry, and Hsien-Hen Lu. 2000. Trends in Cohabitation and Implications for Children's Family Contexts in the United States. *Population Studies* 54 (1):29–41.

Bureau of Justice Statistics. 1993. Survey of Inmates of State Correctional Facilities, 1991. US Department of Commerce, Bureau of the Census. Ann Arbor, MI: Inter-university Consortium for Political and Social Research (producer and distributor).

———. 1994. Survey of Inmates of State Correctional Facilities, 1986. US Department of Commerce, Bureau of the Census. Ann Arbor, MI: Inter-university Consortium for Political and Social Research (producer and distributor).

———. 1997. Survey of Inmates of State and Federal Correctional Facilities, 1979. US Department of Commerce, Bureau of the Census. Ann Arbor, MI: Inter-university Consortium for Political and Social Research (producer and distributor).

———. 2004a. Survey of Inmates of Federal Correctional Facilities, 1991. US Department of Commerce, Bureau of the Census. Ann Arbor, MI: Inter-university Consortium for Political and Social Research (producer and distributor).

———. 2004b. National Corrections Reporting Program, 1982–2002. US Department of Commerce, Bureau of the Census. Ann Arbor, MI: Inter-university Consortium for Political and Social Research (producer and distributor)

———. 2007. Survey of Inmates of State and Federal Correctional Facilities, 2004. US Department of Commerce, Bureau of the Census. Ann Arbor, MI: Inter-university Consortium for Political and Social Research (producer and distributor).

———. National Crime Victimization Survey Violent Crime Trends, 1973-2008. December 4, 2011 2011 [cited December 4, 2011. Available from http://bjs.ojp.usdoj.gov/content/glance/tables/viortrdtab.cfm.

Bureau of Labor Statistics, US Department of Labor. 2011. News Release: The Employment Situation—August 2011. Available online at http://www.bls.gov/news.release/pdf/empsit.pdf.

Callaghan, William M., Marian F. MacDorman, Sonja A. Rasmussen, Cheng Qin, and Eve M. Lackritz. 2006. The Contribution of Preterm Birth to Infant Mortality Rates in the United States. *Pediatrics* 118:1566–1573.

Carlson, Marcia J., and Katherine A Magnuson. 2011. Low-Income Fathers' Influence on Children. *Annals of the American Academy of Political and Social Science* 635:95–116.

Carson, E. Ann, and William J. Sabol. 2012. Prisoners in 2011. Edited by U. S. Department of Justice. Washington, DC: Bureau of Justice Statistics.

Centers for Disease Control and Prevention. 2011. *How Many Children Have Autism?* Centers for Disease Control and Prevention 2010 [cited December 2, 2011]. Available from http://www.cdc.gov/ncbddd/features/counting-autism.html.

Cherlin, Andrew J. 1999. Going to Extremes: Family Structure, Children's Well-Being, and Social Science. *Demography* 36 (4):421–428.

Cho, Rosa M. 2009a. The Impact of Maternal Imprisonment on Children's Probability of Grade Retention: Results from Chicago Public Schools. *Journal of Urban Economics* 65:11–23.

———. 2009b. The Impact of Maternal Incarceration on Children's Educational Achievement: Results from Chicago Public Schools. *Journal of Human Resources* 44:772–797.

Choi, Jeong-Kyun, and Aurora P. Jackson. 2011. Fathers' Involvement and Child Behavior Problems in Poor African American Single-Mother Families. *Children and Youth Services Review* 33 (5):698–704.

Chomitz, Virginia R., Lillian W. Y. Cheung, and Ellice Lieberman. 1995. The Role of Lifestyle in Preventing Low Birth Weight. *Future of Children* 5:121–138.

Clarke, Jennifer G., and Eli Y. Adashi. 2011. Perinatal Care for Incarcerated Patients: A 25-Year-Old Woman Pregnant in Jail. *Journal of the American Medical Association* 305 (9):923–929.

Clear, Todd R. 2007. *Imprisoning Communities: How Mass Incarceration Makes Disadvantaged Neighborhoods Worse.* New York: Oxford University Press.

Cohen, George J. 2002. Helping Children and Families Deal with Divorce and Separation. *Pediatrics* 110 (5):1019–1023.

Comfort, Megan. 2007. Punishment Beyond the Legal Offender. *Annual Review of Law and Social Science* 3 (1):271–284.

———. 2008. *Doing Time Together: Love and Family in the Shadow of the Prison.* Chicago: University of Chicago Press.

Conley, Dalton, and Kristen W. Springer. 2001. Welfare State and Infant Mortality. *American Journal of Sociology* 107:768–807.

Cook, Phillip J., and Jens Ludwig. 2012. More Prisoners versus More Crime is the Wrong Question. In Brookings Policy Brief Series. Washington, DC: The Brookings Institution.

Coontz, Stephanie. 1997. *The Way We Really Are: Coming to Terms with America's Changing Families.* New York: Basic Books.

Couch, Kenneth A., and Robert W. Fairlie. 2010. Last Hired, First Fired? Black-White Unemployment and the Business Cycle. *Demography* 47 (1):227–247.

Culhane, Dennis P., and Stephen Metraux. 1999. One-Year Rates of Public Shelter Utilization by Race/Ethnicity, Age, Sex, and Poverty Status for New York City (1990 and 1995) and Philiadelphia (1995). *Population Research and Policy Review* 18 (3):219–236.

Cummings, E. Mark, and Patrick T. Davis. 1994. Maternal Depression and Child Development. *Journal of Child Psychology* 35 (1):73–112.

Craigie, Terry-Ann L. 2011. The Effect of Paternal Incarceration on Early Child Behavioral Problems. *Journal of Ethnicity in Criminal Justice* 9 (3): 179–199.

Dallaire, Danielle H., Anne Ciccone, and Laura C. Wilson. 2010. Teachers' Experiences With and Expectations of Children with Incarcerated Parents. *Journal of Applied Developmental Psychology* 31 (4):281–290.

Demo, David H., and Martha J. Cox. 2000. Families with Young Children: A Review of Research in the 1990s. *Journal of Marriage and the Family* 62:876–895.

Doyle Jr., Joseph J. 2007. Child Protection and Child Outcomes: Measuring the Effects of Foster Care. *American Economic Review* 97 (5):1583–1610.

———. 2008. Child Protection and Adult Crime: Using Investigator Assignment to Estimate Causal Effects of Foster Care. *Journal of Political Economy* 116 (4):746–770.

Duncan, Greg J., and Jeanne Brooks-Gunn. 1997. *Consequences of Growing Up Poor*. New York: Russell Sage Foundation.

Duncan, Greg J., Katherine A Magnuson, Ariel Kalil, and Kathleen Ziol-Guest. 2011. The Importance of Early Childhood Poverty. *Social Indicators Research*.

Duncan, Otis D., David L. Featherman, and Beverly Duncan. 1972. *Socioeconomic Background and Achievement*. Oxford: Seminar Press.

Durlauf, Steven N., and Daniel S. Nagin. 2011. Imprisonment and Crime. *Criminology & Public Policy* 10 (1):13–54.

Earls, Felton J., Jeanne Brooks-Gunn, Stephen W. Raudenbush, and Robert J. Sampson. 2002. Project on Human Development in Chicago Neighborhoods (PHDCN). Ann Arbor, MI: Inter-university Consortium for Poltical and Social Research (distributor).

Edin, Kathryn. 2000. Few Good Men: Why Low-Income Single Mothers Don't Get Married. *American Prospect* 11 (4):26–31.

Elder, Glen H., Jr. 1974, 1999. *Children of the Great Depression: Social change in life experience*. 25th anniversary ed. Boulder, CO: Westview Press.

Ellwood, John W., and Joshua Guetzkow. 2009. Footing the Bill: Causes and Budgetary Consequences of State Spending on Corrections. In *Do Prisons Make Us Safer?*, edited by S. Raphael and M. A. Stoll. New York: Russell Sage Foundation.

Entwisle, D. R., and K. L. Alexander. 1993. Entry into School: The Beginning School Transition and Educational Stratification in the United-States. *Annual Review of Sociology* 19:401–423.

Farrington, David P. 1994. Cambridge Study in Delinquent Development [Great Britain], 1961–1981 [computer file]. Ann Arbor, MI: Inter-university Consortium for Political and Social Research [distributor].

Fomby, Paula, and Andrew J. Cherlin. 2007. Family Instability and Child Well-Being. *American Sociological Review* 72 (2):181–204.

Foster, Holly, and John Hagan. 2007. Incarceration and Intergenerational Social Exclusion. *Social Problems* 54 (4):399–433.

———. 2009. The Mass Incarceration of Parents in America: Issues of Race/Ethnicity, Collateral Damage to Children, and Prisoner Reentry. *Annals of the American Academy of Political and Social Science* 623 (1):179–194.

Frisbie, W. Parker. 2005. Infant Mortality. In *Handbook of Population*, edited by Dudley L. Poston and Michael Micklin. New York: Kluwer Academic/Plenum.

Frisbie, W. Parker, Monique Biegler, Peter de Turk, Douglas Forbes, and Starling G. Pullum. 1997. Racial and Ethnic Differences in Determinants of Intrauterine Growth Retardation and Other Compromised Birth Outcomes. *American Journal of Public Health* 87:1977–1983.

Frisbie, W. Parker, Seung-Eun Song, Daniel A. Powers, and Julie A. Street. 2004. The Increasing Racial Disparity in Infant Mortality: Respiratory Distress Syndrome and Other Causes. *Demography* 41 (4):773–800.

Gabel, Katherine, and Denise Johnston, eds. 1998. *Children of Incarcerated Parents*. Lanham: Lexington Books.

Geller, Amanda. Forthcoming. Paternal Incarceration and Father-Child Contact in Fragile Families. *Journal of Marriage and the Family*.

Geller, Amanda, Carey E. Cooper, Irwin Garfinkel, Ofira Schwartz-Soicher, and Ronald B. Mincy. 2012. "Beyond Absenteeism: Father Incarceration and Child Development." *Demography* 49 (1): 49–76.

Geller, Amanda, and Marah A. Curtis. 2011. A Sort of Homecoming: Incarceration and Housing Insecurity of Urban Men. *Social Science Research* 40:1196–1213.

Geller, Amanda, Irwin Garfinkel, Carey Cooper, and Ronald Mincy. 2009. Parental Incarceration and Childhood Wellbeing: Implications for Urban Families. *Social Science Quarterly* 90:1186–1202.

Geller, Amanda, Irwin Garfinkel, and Bruce Western. 2011. Paternal Incarceration and Support for Children in Fragile Families. *Demography* 48 (1):25–47.

Gilbert, Brenda C., Holly B. Shulman, Laurie A. Fischer, and Mary M. Rogers. 1999. The Pregnancy Risk Assessment Monitoring System (PRAMS): Methods and 1996 Response Rates from 11 States. *Maternal and Child Health Journal* 3:199–209.

Giordano, Peggy. 2010. *Legacies of Crime: A Follow-Up of Children of Highly Delinquent Girls and Boys*. New York: Cambridge University Press.

Glaze, Lauren E., and Thomas P. Bonczar. 2009. Probation and Parole in the United States, 2008. edited by Bureau of Justice Statistics. Washington, DC: US Government Printing Office.

Glueck, Sheldon and Eleanor Glueck. 1950. *Unraveling Juvenile Delinquency*. Cambridge, MA: Harvard University Press, 1950.

Goffman, Alice. 2009. On the Run: Wanted Men in a Philadelphia Ghetto. *American Sociological Review* 74:339–357.

Gortmaker, Steven L., and Paul H. Wise. 1997. The First Injustice: Socioeconomic Disparities, Health Services Technology, and Infant Mortality. *Annual Review of Sociology* 23 (1):147–170.

Gottfredson, Michael R., and Travis Hirschi. 1990. *A General Theory of Crime*. Palo Alto, CA: Stanford University Press.

Gowan, Teresa. 2002. The Nexus: Homelessness and Incarceration in Two American Cities. *Ethnography* 3:500–534.

Greenberg, David F., and Valerie West. 2001. State Prison Populations and Their Growth, 1971–1991. *Criminology* 39:615–654.

Grieger, Lloyd D., and Sheldon H. Danzinger. 2011. Who Receives Food Stamps during Adulthood? Analyzing Repeatable Events with Incomplete Event Histories. *Demography* 48 (4):1601–1614.

Grinstead, Olga, Bonnie Faigeles, Carrie Bancroft, and Barry Zack. 2001. The Financial Costs of Maintaining Relationships with Incarcerated African American Men: A Survey of Women Prison Visitors. *Journal of African American Men* 6 (1):59–69.

Grogger, Jeffrey T. 1995. The Effect of Arrests on the Employment and Earnings of Young Men. *Quarterly Journal of Economics* 110 (1):51–72.

Grusky, David B., Manwai C. Ku, and Szonja Szelényi. 2008. *Social Stratification: Class, Race, and Gender in Sociological Perspective*. 3rd ed. Boulder, CO: Westview Press.

Guetzkow, Joshua. 2011. Bars versus Butter: The Prison-Welfare Tradeoff and Its Political Underpinnings. Unpublished Manuscript.

Guggenheim, M. 2000. Somebody's Children: Sustaining the Family's Place in Child Welfare Policy. *Harvard Law Review* 113 (7):1716–1750.

Haddad, Maryam B., Todd W. Wilson, Kashef Ijaz, Suzanne M. Marks, and Marisa Moore. 2005. Tuberculosis and Homelessness in the United States: 1994–2003. *Journal of the American Medical Association* 293 (22):2762–2766.

Hagan, John, and Juleigh Petty Coleman. 2001. Returning Captives of the American War on Drugs: Issues of Community and Family Reentry. *Crime and Delinquency* 47 (4):352–367.

Hagan, John, and Holly Foster. 2012. Intergenerational Educational Effects of Mass Imprisonment. *Sociology of Education* 83 (3):259–286.

Hagan, John, and Bill McCarthy. 1997. *Mean Streets: Youth Crime and Homelessness.* Cambridge: Cambridge University Press.

Hagan, John, and Alberto Palloni. 1990. The Social Reproduction of a Criminal Class in Working Class London, circa 1950–1980. *American Journal of Sociology* 96 (2):265–299.

Hagan, John, and Blair Wheaton. 1993. The Search for Adolescent Role Exits and the Transition to Adulthood. *Social Forces* 71 (4):955–980.

Harris, Alexes, Heather Evans, and Katherine Beckett. 2010. Drawing Blood from Stones: Legal Debt and Social Inequality in the Contemporary United States. *American Journal of Sociology* 115 (6):1753–1799.

Harris, K. M., C. T. Halpern, E. Whitsel, J. Hussey, J. Tabor, P. Entzel, and J. R. Udry. 2009. The National Longitudinal Study of Adolescent Health: Research Design. http://www.cpc.unc.edu/projects/addhealth/design.

Hawken, Angela, and Mark Kleinman. 2009. Managing Drug Involved Probationers with Swift and Certain Sanctions: Evaluating Hawaii's HOPE. Washington, DC: National Institute of Justice.

Heckman, James J. 2006. Skills Formation and the Economics of Investing in Disadvantaged Children. *Science* 312:1900–1902.

Heclo, Hugh H. 1997. Values Underpinning Poverty Programs for Children. *The Future of Children* 7 (2):141–148.

Heron, Melonie, Donna L. Hoyert, Sherry L. Murphy, Jiaquan Xu, Kenneth D. Kochanek, and Betzaida Tejada-Vera. 2009. Deaths: Final Data for 2006. In *National Vital Statistics Reports.* Hyattsville, MD: National Center for Health Statistics.

Hirschi, Travis. 1969. *Causes of Delinquency.* Berkeley: University of California Press.

Holzer, Harry J. 2010. Testimony before the U.S. Senate Subcommittee on Children and Famies on the "Great Recession" and the Well-Being of American Children. Washington, DC: Urban Institute.

Hopper, Kim. 2003. *Reckoning with Homelessness.* Ithaca, NY: Cornell University Press.

Hoyert, Donna L., T. J. Mathews, Fay Menacker, Donna M. Strobino, and Bernard Guyer. 2006. Annual Summary of Vital Statistics: 2004. *Pediatrics* 117:168–183.

Huebner, Beth M. and Regan Gustafson. 2007. The Effect of Maternal Incarceration on Adult Offspring Involvement in the Criminal Justice System. *Journal of Criminal Justice* 35:283–296.

Hummer, Robert A., Daniel A. Powers, Starling G. Pullum, Ginger L. Gossman, and W. Parker Frisbie. 2007. Paradox Found (Again): Infant Mortality among the Mexican-Origin Population of the United States. *Demography* 44:441–457.

Jencks, Christopher. 1994. *The Homeless*. Cambridge, MA: Harvard University Press.

Johnson, Elizabeth I. and Beth Easterling. 2012. Understanding the Unique Effects of Parental Incarceration on Children: Challenges, Progress, and Recommendations. *Journal of Marriage and the Family* 74 (2):342–356.

Johnson, Elizabeth I., and Jane Waldfogel. 2004. Children of Incarcerated Parents: Multiple Risks and Children's Living Arrangements. In *Imprisoning America: The Social Effects of Mass Incarceration*, edited by M. E. Patillo, D. F. Weiman, and B. Western. New York: Russell Sage Foundation.

———. 2002. Parental Incarceration: Recent Trends and Implications for Child Welfare. *Social Services Review* 76:460–479.

Johnson, Rucker, and Steven Raphael. 2009. The Effects of Male Incarceration Dynamics on Acquired Immune Deficiency Syndrome Infection Rates among African American Women and Men. *Journal of Law and Economics* 52:251–293.

———. 2012. How Much Crime Reduction Does the Marginal Prisoner Buy? *Journal of Law and Economics* 55 (2):275–310.

Johnston, Denise. 2006. The Wrong Road: Efforts to Understand the Effects of Parental Crime and Incarceration. *Criminology & Public Policy* 5 (4):703–719.

———. 1995. Effects of Parental Incarceration. In *Children of Incarcerated Parents*, edited by Katherine Gabel and Denise Johnston (pp. 59–88). New York: Lexington.

Jones, Loring P. 1988. The Effect of Unemployment on Children and Adolescents. *Children and Youth Services Review* 10 (3):199–215.

Kiernan, Kathleen E., and Andrew J. Cherlin. 1999. Parental Divorce and Partnership Dissolution in Adulthood: Evidence from a British Cohort Study. *Population Studies* 53 (1):39–48.

Kerker, Bonnie D., Jay Bainbridge, Joseph Kennedy, Yussef Bennani, Tracy Agerton, Dova Marder, Lisa Forgione, Andrew Faciano, and Lorna E. Thorpe. 2011. A Population-Based Assessment of the Health of Homeless Families in New York City, 2001–2003. *American Journal of Public Health* 101 (3):546–553.

Kessler, Ronald C., Patricia Berglund, Olga Demler, Robert Jin, Doreen Koretz, Kathleen R. Merikangas, A. John Rush, Ellen E. Walters, and Philip S. Wang. 2003. The Epidemiology of Major Depressive Disorder. *Journal of the American Medical Association* 289 (23):3095–3105.

Khan, Maria R., Irene A. Doherty, Victor J. Schoenbach, Eboni M. Taylor, Matthew W. Epperson, and Adaora A. Adimora. 2009. Incarceration and High-Risk Sex Partnerships among Men in the United States. *Journal of Urban Health* 86 (4):584–601.

King, Valerie. 1994. Nonresident Father Involvement and Child Well-Being: Can Dads Make a Difference? *Journal of Family Issues* 15 (1):78–96.

Kinner S. A., Alati R., Najman J. M., and Williams G. M. 2007. Do Paternal Arrest and Imprisonment Lead to Child Behavior Problems and Substance Use? A Longitudinal Analysis. *Journal of Child Psychology and Psychiatry* 48:1148–1156.

Kling, Jeffrey. 2006. Incarceration Length, Employment and Earnings. *American Economic Review* 96 (3):863–876.

Kochhar, Rakesh, Richard Fry, and Paul Taylor. 2011. Twenty-to-One: Wealth Gaps Rise to Record Highs between Whites, Blacks, and Hispanics. Washington, DC: Pew Research Center. Available online at http://pewsocialtrends.org/files/2011/07/SDT-Wealth-Report_7-26-11_FINAL.pdf.

Kotelchuck, Milton. 1994. An Evaluation of the Kessner Adequacy of Prenatal Care Index and a Proposed Adequacy of Prenatal Care Utilization Index. *American Journal of Public Health* 84:1414–1420.

Kramer, Michale S., Louis Seguin, John Lydon, and Lise Goulet. 2000. Socioeconomic Disparities in Pregnancy Outcome: Why Do the Poor Fare So Poorly? *Paediatric and Perinatal Epidemiology* 14:194–201.

Kruttschnitt, Candace. 2010. The Paradox of Women's Imprisonment. *Daedalus* 139 (3):32–42.

Kushel, M. B., E. Vittinghoff, and J. S. Haas. 2001. Factors Associated with the Health Care Utilization of Homeless Persons. *Journal of the American Medical Association* 285 (2):200–206.

Lareau, Annette. 2003. *Unequal Childhoods: Class, Race, and Family Life.* Berkeley: University of California Press.

Lee, Barrett A., Kimberly A. Tyler, and James D. Wright. 2010. The New Homelessness Revisited. *Annual Review of Sociology* 36:501–521.

Lee, Hedwig, and Christopher Wildeman. 2013. Things Fall Apart: Heath Consequences of Mass Imprisonment for African American Women. *Review of Black Political Economy* 40:39-52

Lee, Hedwig, Christopher Wildeman, Emily A. Wang, Nikki Matsuko, and James S. Jackson. Forthcoming. A Heavy Burden? The Cardiovascular Health Consequences of Having a Family Member Incarcerated. *American Journal of Public Health.*

Levitt, Steven. 1996. The Effect of Prison Population Size on Crime: Evidence from Prison Overcrowding and Litigation. *Quarterly Journal of Economics* 111:319–351.

Lichter, Daniel. 1997. Poverty and Inequality Among Children. *Annual Review of Sociology* 23:121–145.

Liebow, Elliott. (1967) 2003. *Tally's Corner: A Study of Negro Streetcorner Men.* Lanham, MD: Rowan and Littlefield.

Link, Bruce G., and Jo Phelan. 1995. Social Conditions as Fundamental Causes of Disease. *Journal of Health and Social Behavior* 35 (extra issue):80–94.

———. 2002. McKeown and the Idea that Social Conditions Are Fundamental Causes of Disease. *American Journal of Public Health* 92:730–732.

Loeber, R., and D. Hay. 1997. Key Issues in the Development of Aggression and Violence from Childhood to Early Adulthood. *Annual Review of Psychology* 48:371–410.

Lopoo, Leonard M., and Bruce Western. 2005. Incarceration and the Formation and Stability of Marital Unions. *Journal of Marriage and the Family* 67 (3):721–734.

Lovell, Phillip, and Julia B. Isaacs. 2010. Families of the Recession: Unemployed Parents and Their Children. Washington, DC: First Focus Campaign for Children.

MacDorman, Marian F., Joyce Martin, T. J. Mathews, Donna Hoyert, and Stephenie Ventura. 2005. Explaining the 2001-02 Infant Mortality Increase: Data from the Linked Birth/Infant Death Data Set. In National Vital Statistics Reports. Hyattsville, MD: National Center for Health Statistics.

Maguire, Kathleen, and Ann L. Pastore, eds. 2001. Sourcebook of Criminal Justice Statistics: Available online at http://www.albany.edu/sourcebook/archive.html.

Mannuzza, Salvatore, Rachel G. Klein, Abrah Bessler, Patricia Malloy, and Mary E. Hynes. 1997. Educational and Occupational Outcome of Hyperactive Boys Grown Up. Journal of the American Academy of Child & Adolescent Psychiatry 36 (9):1222-1227.

Manza, Jeff, and Christopher Uggen. 2006. Locked Out: Felon Disenfranchisement and American Democracy. New York: Oxford University Press.

Martinson, Robert. 1974. What Works? Questions and Answers about Prison Reform. Public Interest (35):22-54.

Massoglia, Michael. 2008. Incarceration as Exposure: The Prison, Infectious Disease, and Other Stress-Related Illnesses. Journal of Health and Social Behavior 49 (1):56-71.

Massoglia, Michael, Brianna Remster, and Ryan D. King. 2011. Stigma or Separation? Understanding the Incarceration-Divorce Relationship. Social Forces 90 (1):133-155.

Mathews, T. J., and Marian F. MacDorman. 2007. Infant Mortality Statistics from the 2004 Period Linked Birth/Infant Death Data Set. In National Vital Statistics Reports. Hyattsville, MD: National Center for Health Statistics.

McLanahan, Sara, and Christine Percheski. 2008. Family Structure and the Reproduction of Inequalities. Annual Review of Sociology 34 (1):257-276.

McLanahan, Sara, and Gary Sandefur. 1994. Growing Up with a Single Parent: What Hurts, What Helps. Cambridge, MA: Harvard University Press.

McLanahan, Sara, Laura Tach, and Daniel Schnieder. Forthcoming. The Causal Effects of Father Absence. Annual Review of Sociology 39.

McLeod, Jane D., and Karen Kaiser. 2004. Childhood Emotional and Behavioral Problems and Educational Attainment. *American Sociological Review* 69 (5):636–658.

McLeod, Jane D., and James Nonnemaker. 2000. Poverty and Child Emotional and Behavioral Problems: Racial/Ethnic Differences in Processes and Effects. *Journal of Health and Social Behavior* 41 (2):137–161.

McLeod, Jane D., and Michael J. Shanahan. 1993. Poverty, Parenting, and Childrens Mental-Health. *American Sociological Review* 58 (3):351–366.

Menaghan, Elizabeth G. 1997. The Intergenerational Costs of Parental Social Stressors: Academic and Social Difficulties in Early Adolescence for Children of Young Mothers. *Journal of Health and Social Behavior* 38 (1):72–86.

Moffitt, Terrie E. 1993. Adolescence-Limited and Life-Course-Persistent Antisocial-Behavior:A Developmental Taxonomy. *Psychological Review* 100 (4):674–701.

Moss, Nancy E., and Carver, Karen. 1998. The Effect of WIC and Medicaid on Infant Mortality in the United States. *American Journal of Public Health* 88:1354–1361.

Muller, Christopher. 2012. Northward Migration and the Rise of Racial Disparity in American Incarceration, 1880-1950. *American Journal of Sociology* 118 (2):281–326.

Mumola, Christopher J. 2000. Incarcerated Parents and Their Children. Washington, DC: Bureau of Justice Statistics. US Government Printing Office.

Murray, Joseph, and David P. Farrington. 2005. Parental Imprisonment: Effects on Boys' Antisocial Behavior and Deliquency Throughout the Life-Course. *Journal of Children Psychology and Psychiatry* 46:1269–1278.

———. 2008. Parental Imprisonment: Long-lasting Effects on Boys Internalizing Problems through the Life-Course. *Development and Psychopathology* 20:273–290.

Murray, Joseph, David P. Farrington, and Ivana Sekol. 2012a. Children's Anti-Social Behavior, Mental Health, Drug Use, and Educational Performance after Parental Incarceration: A Systematic Review and Meta-Analysis. *Psychological Bulletin* 138 (2):175–210.

Murray, Joseph, Loeber, Rolf, and Dustin Pardini. 2012b. Parental Involvement in the Criminal Justice System and the Development of Youth Theft, Marijuana Use, Depression, and Poor Academic Performance. *Criminology* 50 (1):255–302.

Nagin, Daniel, and Richard Tremblay. 2001. Parental and Early Childhood Predictors of Persistent Physical Aggression in Boys from Kindergarten to High School. *Archives of General Psychiatry* 58:389–94.

National Association for Gifted Children. 2011. *Frequently Asked Questions 2008* [cited December 2, 2011]. Available from http://www.nagc.org/index2.aspx?id=548.

National Center on Family Homelessness. 2009. America's Youngest Outcasts: State Report Card on Child Homelessness. Needham, MA: American Institutes for Research.

———. 2011. America's Youngest Outcasts: State Report Card on Child Homelessness, 2010. Needham, MA: American Institutes for Research.

Nesmith, Ande, and Ebony Ruhland. 2008. Children of Incarcerated Parents: Challenges and Resiliency, in Their Words. *Children and Youth Services Review* 30:1119–1130.

Nurse, Anne. 2002. *Fatherhood Arrested: Parenting from within the Juvenile Justice System*. Nashville, TN: Vanderbilt University Press.

Nye, Ivan. 1958. *Family Relationships and Delinquent Behavior*. New York: John Wiley and Sons.

OECD. 2006. OECD Health Data, 2006. OECD, Paris.

Page, Joshua. 2011. *The Toughest Beat: Politics, Punishment, and the Prison Officers' Union in California*. New York: Oxford University Press.

Pager, Devah. 2003. The Mark of a Criminal Record. *American Journal of Sociology* 108 (5):937–975.

Pampel, Fred C., and Pillai, Vijayan K. 1986. Patterns and Determinants of Infant Mortality in Developed Nations, 1950-1975. *Demography* 23:525–542.

Pastore, Ann L., and Kathleen Maguire, eds. 2003. *Sourcebook of Criminal Justice Statistics*: Available online at http://www.albany.edu/sourcebook.

Petersilia, Joan. 2003. *When Prisoners Come Home: Parole and Prisoner Reentry.* New York: Oxford University Press.

Pettit, Becky. 2012. *Invisible Men: Mass Incarceration and the Myth of Black Progress.* New York: Russell Sage Foundation.

Pettit, Becky, and Christopher Lyons. 2007. Status and the Stigma of Incarceration: The Labor-Market Effects of Incarceration by Race, Class, and Criminal Involvement. In *Barriers to Reentry: The Labor Market for Released Prisoners in Post-Industrial America*, edited by S. Bushway, M. Stoll, and D. Weiman. New York: Russell Sage Foundation.

Pettit, Becky, and Bruce Western. 2004. Mass Imprisonment and the Life Course: Race and Class Inequality in U.S. Incarceration. *American Sociological Review* 69:151–169.

Poehlmann, Julie. 2005. Representations of attachment relationships in children of incarcerated mothers. *Child Development* 76:679–696.

Rafferty, Y., M. Shinn, and B. Weitzman. 2004. Academic Achievement among Formerly Homeless Adolescents and Their Continually Housed Peers. *Journal of School Psychology* 42:179–199.

Rank, Mark Robert. 2005. *One Nation, Underprivileged: Why American Poverty Affects Us All.* New York: Oxford University Press.

Rank, Mark Robert, and Thomas A. Hirschl. 1999. The Economic Risk of Childhood in America: Estimating the Probability of Poverty across the Formative Years. *Journal of Marriage and Family* 61 (4):1058–1067.

Raphael, Steven, and David Weiman. 2007. The Impact of Local Labor Market Conditions on the Likelihood That Parolees Are Returned to Custody. In *Barriers to Reentry: The Labor Market for Released Prisoners in Post-Industrial America*, edited by S. Bushway, M. Stoll, and D. Weiman. New York: Russell Sage Foundation.

Reckless, Walter. 1961. A New Theory of Delinquency and Crime. *Federal Probation* 25:42–46.

Reichman, Nancy, Julien Teitler, Irwin Garfinkel, and Sara McLanahan. 2001. Fragile Families: Sample and Design. *Children and Youth Services Review* 23:303–326.

Roettger, Michael E., and Jason D. Boardman. 2012. Parental Incarceration and Gender-Based Risks for Increased BMI: Evidence from a Longitudinal Study of Adolescents and Young Adults in the United States. *American Journal of Epidemiology* 175 (7):636–644.

Roettger, Michael E., and Raymond R. Swisher. 2011. Associations of Father's History of Incarceration with Delinquency and Arrest among Black, White, and Hispanic Males in the U.S. *Criminology* 49 (4):1109–1147.

Roettger, Michael E., Raymond R. Swisher, Danielle C. Kuhl, and Jorge Chavez. 2011. Parental Incarceration and Trajectories of Drug Use from Adolescence to Young Adulthood. *Addiction* 106:121–132.

Rosenbaum, Paul R., and Donald B. Rubin. 1983. The Central Role of the Propensity Score in Observational Studies for Causal Effects. *Biometrika* 70 (1):41–55.

Rugh, Jacob S., and Douglas S. Massey. 2010. Racial Segregation and the American Foreclosure Crisis. *American Sociological Review* 75:629–651.

Ruhm, Christopher J. 2000. Are Recessions Good for Your Health? *Quarterly Journal of Economics* 115:617–650.

Rutter, Michael. 1972. *Maternal Deprivation*. Middlesex, England: Penguin Books.

Sabol, William J., Heather C. West, and Matthew Cooper. 2009. Prisoners in 2008. Bureau of Justice Statistics Bulletin. Washington DC: US Government Printing Office.

Sack, William 1977. Children of Imprisoned Fathers. *Psychiatry* 40:163–174.

Sampson, Robert J. 2011. The Incarceration Ledger: Toward a New Era in Assessing Societal Consequences. *Criminology & Public Policy* 10:819–828.

Sampson, Robert J. and John Laub. 1993. *Crime in the Making: Pathways and Turning Points Through Life*. Cambridge, MA: Harvard University Press.

Sampson, Robert J., and Charles Loeffler. 2010. Punishment's Place: The Local Concentration of Mass Incarceration. *Daedalus* 139:20–31.

Schempf, Ashley H., Amy M. Branum, Susan L. Lukacs, and Kenneth C. Schoendorf. 2007. The Contribution of Preterm Birth to the Black-White Infant Mortality Gap, 1990 and 2000. *American Journal of Public Health* 97 (7):1255–1260.

Schnittker, Jason, and Andrea John. 2007. Enduring Stigma: The Long-Term Effects of Incarceration on Health. *Journal of Health and Social Behavior* 48 (2):115–130.

Schwartz-Soicher, Ofira, Amanda Geller, and Irwin Garfinkel. 2011. The Effect of Paternal Incarceration on Material Hardship. *Social Service Review* (3):447–473.

Schweinhart, Lawrence J., Jeanne Montie, Zongping Xiang, William S. Barnett, Clive R. Belfield, and Milagros Nores. 2005. *Lifetime Effects: The HighScope Perry Preschool Study through Age 40.* Ypsilanti, MI: High/Scope Press.

Sharkey, Patrick. 2010. The Acute Effect of Local Homicides on Children's Cognitive Performance. *Proceedings of the National Academy of Sciences* 107:11733–11738.

Sherman, Lawrence W., Denise C. Gottfredson, Doris L. MacKenzie, John Eck, Peter Reuter, and Shawn Bushway. 1998. Preventing Crime: What Works, What Doesn't, What's Promising. Washington, DC: US Department of Justice, National Institute of Justice.

Siegel, Jane. 2011. *Disrupted Childhoods: Children of Women in Prison.* Series in Childhood Studies. New Brunswick, NJ: Rutgers University Press.

Sik Kim, Hyun. 2011. Consequences of Parental Divorce for Child Development. *American Sociological Review* 76 (3):487–511.

Simon, Jonathan. 2007. *Governing through Crime: How the War on Crime Transformed American Democracy and Created a Culture of Fear.* New York: Oxford University Press.

Singh, Gopal K., and Kogan, Michael D. 2007. Persistent Socioeconomic Disparities in Infant, Neonatal, and Postneonatal Mortality Rates in the United States, 1969-2001. *Pediatrics* 119:e929–939.

Sourcebook of Criminal Justice Statistics. 2011. Table 6.0001.2009: Estimated Number and Percent Distribution of Prisoners under Jurisdiction of State Correctional Authorities. Albany, NY: Sourcebook of Criminal Justice Statistics online. http://www.albany.edu/sourcebook/.

South, Scott J. 2002. The Variable Effects of Family Background on the Transition to Marriage: United States, 1969-1993. *Social Science Research* 30 (4):606–626.

Spaulding, Anne C., Ryan M. Seals, Victoria A. McCallum, Sebastian D. Perez, Amanda K. Brzozowski, and N. Kyle Steenland. 2011. Prisoner Survival Inside and Outside of the Institution: Implications for Health-Care Planning. *American Journal of Epidemiology* 173:479–487.

Stack, Carol. 1974. *All Our Kin.* New York: Basic Books.

Stanton, Ann M. 1980. *When Mothers Go to Jail.* Lexington, MA: Lexington Books.

Staveteig, Sarah, and Alyssa Wigton. 2000. Racial and Ethnic Disparities: Key Findings from the National Survey of America's Families. In *New Federalism: National Survey of America's Families.* Washington, DC: Urban Institute.

Sugie, Naomi. 2012. Punishment and Welfare: Paternal Incarceration and Families' Receipt of Public Assistance. *Social Forces* 90 (4):1403–1427.

Sutherland, Edwin H., and Donald R. Cressey. 1978. *Criminology.* 9th edition. New York: J. B. Lippincott.

Swann, Christopher, and Michelle Sheran Sylvester. 2006. The Foster Care Crisis: What Caused Caseloads to Grow? *Demography* 43 (2):309–335.

Tierney, John. 2013. Prison Population Can Shrink When Police Crowd Streets. *New York Times.*

Trent, Katherine, and Kyle Crowder. 1997. Adolescent Birth Intentions, Social Disadvantage, and Behavioral Outcomes. *Journal of Marriage and Family* 59 (3):523–535.

Turnanovic, Jillian J., Nancy Rodriguez, and Travis C. Pratt. 2012. The Collateral Consequences of Incarceration Revisited: A Qualitative Analysis of the Effects of Caregivers of Children of Incarcerated Parents. *Criminology* 50 (4):913–959.

Turney, Kristin. 2011. Chronic and Proximate Depression among Mothers: Implications for Child Well-Being. *Journal of Marriage and Family* 73 (1):149–163.

Turney, Kristin, Jason Schnittker, and Christopher Wildeman. 2012. Those They Leave Behind: Paternal Incarceration and Maternal Instrumental Support. *Journal of Marriage and the Family* 74 (5):1149–1165.

US Department of Health and Human Services. 1994. Vital Statistics of the United States, 1990. Hyattsville, MD: Centers for Disease Control and Prevention, National Center for Health Statistics.

US Department of Health and Human Services, Administration for Children and Families, Administration on Children, Youth and Families, Children's Bureau. 2009. The AFCARS Report: Preliinary FY 2009 Estimates as of July 2010. Available online at http://www.acf.hhs.gov/programs/cb/stats_research/afcars/tar/report17.pdf.

US Department of Health and Human Services, National Center for Health Statistics. 1982. Vital Statistics of the United States, 1980: Life Tables. Hyattsville: MD: US Department of Health and Human Services.

———. 1994. VItal Statistics of the United States, 1990: Life Tables. Hyattsville, MD: US Department of Health and Human Services.

US Department of Health and Human Services, National Center for Health Statistics. 2002. Natality Detail File, 1965-1997 [computer files]. Hyattsville, MD: US Department of Health and Human Services [producer], 1969–1998. Ann Arbor: MI: Inter-university Consortium for Political and Social Research (distributor).

US Department of Justice. 2010. *Correctional Populations in the United States, 2009*. Washington, DC: Office of Justice Programs.

Uggen, Christopher, and Sara Wakefield. 2005. Young Adults Reentering the Community from the Criminal Justice System: The Challenge of Becoming an Adult. In *On Your Own Without a Net: The Transition to Adulthood for Vulnerable Populations*, edited by D. W. Osgood, M. Foster, and C. Flanagan. Chicago: University of Chicago Press.

UNICEF. 2012. Measuring Child Poverty: New League Tables of Child Poverty in the World's Richest Countries. Florence: UNICEF Innocenti Research Centre.

Van de Rakt, Marieke, Joseph Murray, and Paul Nieuwbeerta. 2012. The Long-Term Effects of Paternal Imprisonment on Criminal Trajectories of Children. *Journal of Research in Crime and Delinquency* 49 (1):81–108.

Vostanis, P., E. Grattan, and S. Cumella. 1997. Psychosocial Functioning of Homeless Children. *Journal of the American Academy of Child & Adolescent Psychiatry* 36:881–889.

Wakefield, Sara. 2007. *The Consequences of Incarceration for Parents and Children*. Doctoral Dissertation, Department of Sociology, University of Minnesota, Minneapolis, MN.

Wakefield, Sara, and Christopher Uggen. 2010. Incarceration and Stratification. *Annual Review of Sociology* 36 (1):387–406.

Wakefield, Sara, and Christopher Wildeman. 2011. Mass Imprisonment and Racial Disparities in Childhood Behavioral Problems. *Criminology & Public Policy* 10 (3):793–817.

Walmsley, Roy. 2008. World Prison Population List, 7th edition. London: International Centre for Prison Studies.

Weisburd, David, Elizabeth R. Groff, and Sue-Ming Yang. 2012. *The Criminology of Place*. New York: Oxford University Press.

Western, Bruce. 2002. The Impact of Incarceration on Wage Mobility and Inequality. *American Sociological Review* 67:477–498.

———. 2006. *Punishment and Inequality in America*. New York: Russell Sage Foundation.

Western, Bruce, and Becky Pettit. 2010. Collateral Costs: Incarceration's Effect on Economic Mobility. Washington, DC: The Pew Charitable Trusts.

Western, Bruce, and Christopher Wildeman. 2009. The Black Family and Mass Incarceration. *Annals of the American Academy of Political and Social Science* 621 (1):221–242.

Western, Bruce and Christopher Muller. 2013. "Mass Incarceration, Macrosociology, and the Poor." *Annals of the American Academy of Political and Social Science* 647, 1:166–189.

Wilbur M. B., Marani J. E., Appugliese D., Woods R., Siegel J. A., Cabral H. J., and Frank D. 2007. Socioemotional Effects of Fathers' Incarceration on Low-Income, Urban, School-Aged Children. *Pediatrics* 120:678–685.

Wildeman, Christopher. 2009. Parental Imprisonment, the Prison Boom, and the Concentration of Childhood Advantage. *Demography* 46:265–280.

———. 2010. Parental Incarceration and Children's Physically Aggressive Behaviors: Evidence from the Fragile Families and Child Wellbeing Study. *Social Forces* 89:285–310.

———. 2012. Imprisonment and Infant Mortality. *Social Problems* 59 (2):228–259.

———. Forthcoming. Parental Incarceration, Child Homelessness, and the Invisible Consequences of Mass Imprisonment. *Annals of the American Academy of Political and Social Science*.

Wildeman, Christopher, Signe Hald Anderson, Hedwig Lee, and Kristian Kernt Karlson. Forthcoming. Parental Incarceration and Child Mortality in Denmark. *American Journal of Public Health*.

Wildeman, Christopher, and Christopher Muller. 2012. Mass Imprisonment and Inequality in Health and Family Life. *Annual Review of Law and Social Science* 8: 11–30.

Wildeman, Christopher, Jason Schnittker, and Kristin Turney. 2012. Despair by Association? The Mental Health of Mothers with Children by Recently Incarcerated Fathers. *American Sociological Review* 77 (2):216–243.

Wildeman, Christopher, and Kristin Turney. Forthcoming. Positive, Negative, or Null? The Effects of Maternal Incarceration on Children's Behavioral Problems. Demography.

Wildeman, Christopher, Sara Wakefield, and Kristin Turney. 2013. Misidentifying the Effects of Parental Incarceration? A Comment on Johnson and Easterling. *Journal of Marriage and the Family* 75 (1):252–258.

Wildeman, Christopher, and Bruce Western. 2010. Incarceration in Fragile Families. *Future of Children* 20 (2):157–177.

Wilkinson, Richard G. 1992. Income Distribution and Life Expectancy. *British Medical Journal* 304:165–168.

Wilkinson, Richard G., and Pickett, Kate E. 2009. Income Inequality and Social Dysfunction. *Annual Review of Sociology* 35:493–511.

Williams, David R., Hector M. Gonzalez, Harold Neighbors, Randolph Nesse, Jamie M. Abelson, Julie Sweetman, and James S. Jackson. 2007. Prevalence and Distribution of Major Depressive Disorder in African Americans, Caribbean Blacks, and Non-Hispanic Whites: Results from the National Survey of American Life. *Archives of General Psychiatry* 64 (3):305–315.

Winship, Christopher, and Stephen L. Morgan. 1999. The Estimation of Causal Effects from Observational Data. *Annual Review of Sociology* 25 (1):659–706.

Wise, Paul H. 2003. The Anatomy of a Disparity in Infant Mortality. *Annual Review of Public Health* 24 (1):341–362.

Zimring, Franklin E. 2012. *The City That Became Safe: New York's Lessons for Urban Crime and Its Control*. New York: Oxford University Press.

INDEX

Lightning Source UK Ltd.
Milton Keynes UK
UKOW03f1505120317
296411UK00004B/33/P